EKATERINA GORDEEVA

OVERCOMING ADVERSITY

EKATERINA GORDEEVA

Anne E. Hill

Introduction by James Scott Brady,
Trustee, the Center to Prevent Handgun Violence
Vice Chairman, the Brain Injury Foundation

Chelsea House Publishers

Philadelphia

For George, my true companion.

Frontis: Ekaterina Gordeeva has overcome the tragic death of her young husband and skating partner to forge new career paths: professional singles skater, star of television specials, and author of two bestselling books.

CHELSEA HOUSE PUBLISHERS

EDITOR IN CHIEF Stephen Reginald
PRODUCTION MANAGER Pamela Loos
MANAGING EDITOR James D. Gallagher
DIRECTOR OF PHOTOGRAPHY Judy L. Hasday
ART DIRECTOR Sara Davis
SENIOR PRODUCTION EDITOR Lisa Chippendale

Staff for **Ekaterina Gordeeva**
ASSOCIATE ART DIRECTOR Takeshi Takahashi
DESIGNER 21st Century Publishing and Communications, Inc.
PICTURE RESEARCHER Patricia Burns
COVER ILLUSTRATION Gary Maria
COVER DESIGN Brian Wible/Keith Trego

Acknowledgments:
Thanks to Vella Bellaart and Sylvia Yu of the G & G International Fan Club.
Special thanks to Deb Nast and Ekaterina Gordeeva for their time and attention.

www.chelseahouse.com

3 5 7 9 8 6 4 2

Library of Congress Cataloging-in-Publication Data

Hill, Anne E., 1974-
Ekaterina Gordeeva / Anne E. Hill.
    p.   cm. — (Overcoming adversity)
Includes bibliographical references and index.
Summary: A biography of skating star Ekaterina Gordeeva who, with her husband Sergei Grinkov, won two Olympic medals, and who, since his untimely death in 1995, skates alone.
ISBN 0-7910-4848-5 — ISBN 0-7910-4949-3 (pbk.)
1. Gordeeva, Ekaterina—Juvenile literature. 2. Skaters—Russia (Federation)—Biography—Juvenile literature. 3. Grinkov, Sergei, 1967-1995—Juvenile literature. 4. Ice dancing—Russia (Federation)—Juvenile literature. [1. Gordeeva, Ekaterina. 2. Ice skaters. 3. Women—Biography. 4. Grinkov, Sergei, 1967–1995.] I. Title. II. Series.
GV850.G67H55   1998
796.91'2'092—dc21
[b]   98-31348
                                                       CIP
                                                       AC

CONTENTS

OVERCOMING ADVERSITY

TIM ALLEN
comedian/performer

MAYA ANGELOU
author

APOLLO 13 MISSION
astronauts

LANCE ARMSTRONG
professional cyclist

DREW BARRYMORE
actress

DREW CAREY
comedian/performer

JIM CARREY
comedian/performer

BILL CLINTON
U.S. president

TOM CRUISE
actor

MICHAEL J. FOX
actor

WHOOPI GOLDBERG
comedian/performer

EKATERINA GORDEEVA
figure skater

SCOTT HAMILTON
figure skater

JEWEL
singer/songwriter

JAMES EARL JONES
actor

QUINCY JONES
musician and producer

ABRAHAM LINCOLN
U.S. president

WILLIAM PENN
Pennsylvania's founder

JACKIE ROBINSON
baseball legend

ROSEANNE
entertainer

MONICA SELES
tennis star

SAMMY SOSA
baseball star

DAVE THOMAS
entrepreneur

SHANIA TWAIN
entertainer

ROBIN WILLIAMS
performer

BRUCE WILLIS
actor

STEVIE WONDER
entertainer

ON FACING ADVERSITY

James Scott Brady

I GUESS IT'S a long way from a Centralia, Illinois, train yard to the George Washington University Hospital Trauma Unit. My dad was a yardmaster for the old Chicago, Burlington & Quincy Railroad. As a child, I used to get to sit in the engineer's lap and imagine what it was like to drive that train. I guess I always have liked being in the "driver's seat."

Years later, however, my interest turned from driving trains to driving campaigns. In 1979, former Texas governor John Connally hired me as a press secretary in his campaign for the American presidency. We lost the Republican primary to a former Hollywood star named Ronald Reagan. But I managed to jump over to the Reagan campaign. When Reagan was elected in 1980, I was "sitting in the catbird seat," as humorist James Thurber would say—poised to be named presidential press secretary. I held that title throughout the eight years of the Reagan administration. But not without one terrible, extended interruption.

It happened barely two months after the Reagan administration took office. I never even heard the shots. On March 30, 1981, my life went blank in an instant. In an attempt to assassinate President Reagan, John Hinckley Jr. armed himself with a "Saturday night special"—a low-quality, $29 pistol—and shot wildly as our presidential entourage exited a Washington hotel. One of the exploding bullets struck me just above the left eye. It shattered into a couple dozen fragments, some of which penetrated my skull and entered my brain.

The next few months of my life were a nightmare of repeated surgery, broken contact with the outside world, and a variety of medical complications. More than once, I was very close to death.

The next few years were filled with frustrating struggles to function with a paralyzed right side, struggles to speak and communicate.

To people who face and defeat daunting obstacles, "ambition" is not becoming wealthy or famous or winning elections or awards. Words like "ambition" and "achievement" and "success" take on very different meanings. The objective is just to live, to wake up every morning. The goals are not lofty; they are very ordinary.

My own heroes are ordinary folks—but they accomplish extraordinary things because they try. My greatest hero is my wife, Sarah. She's accomplished a lot of things in life, but two stand out. The first has been the way she has cared for me and our son since I was shot. A tremendous tragedy and burden was dropped unexpectedly into her life, totally beyond her control and without justification. She could have given up; instead, she focused her energies on preserving our family and returning our lives to normal as much as possible. Week by week, month by month, year by year, she has not reached for the miraculous, just for the normal. Yet in focusing on the normal, she has helped accomplish the miraculous.

Her other most remarkable accomplishment, to me, has been spearheading the effort to keep guns out of the hands of criminals and children in America. Opponents call her a "gun grabber"; I call her a national hero. And I am not alone.

After a seven-year battle, during which Sarah and I worked tirelessly to educate the public about the need for stronger gun laws, the Brady Bill became law in 1993. It was a victory, achieved in the face of tremendous opposition, that now benefits all Americans. From the time the law took effect through fall 1997, background checks had stopped 173,000 criminals and other high-risk purchasers from buying handguns, and the law has helped to reduce illegal gun trafficking.

Sarah was not pursuing fame, or even recognition. She simply started at one point—when our son, Scott, found a loaded handgun on the seat of a pickup truck and, thinking it was a toy, pointed it at Sarah.

Fortunately, no one was hurt. But seeing a gun nearly bring a second tragedy upon our family, Sarah became determined to do whatever she could to prevent senseless death and injury from guns.

Some people think of Sarah as a powerful political force. To me, she's the person who so many times fed me and helped me dress during my long years of recovery.

Overcoming obstacles is part of life, not just for people who are challenged by disabilities, illnesses, or tragedies, but for all people. No matter what the obstacle—fear, disability, prejudice, grief, or a difficulty that isn't likely to "just go away"—we can all work to make this world a better place.

Ekaterina Gordeeva raises her arms in celebration of her late husband, Sergei Grinkov, during the February 1996 tribute to his life. The 28-year-old Grinkov died suddenly of a heart attack in November 1995 while training with Katia for the show Stars on Ice.

1

A CELEBRATION
OF A LIFE

AS SHE STOOD behind a curtain that separated her from an audience anxious to see her debut performance as a singles skater, Ekaterina Gordeeva had conflicting feelings—loneliness, happiness, fear, excitement. It had been nearly 14 years since she had skated alone. But this February 27, 1996, Stars on Ice performance in Hartford, Connecticut, was perhaps the most significant of her life. Tonight, she skated in memory of her late husband, Sergei Grinkov.

As she waited to glide onto the ice, Gordeeva heard the opening bars of Beethoven's "Moonlight Sonata"—the music she and Sergei had skated to when they won their second Olympic gold medal. Gordeeva remembered how before every routine they skated, she and Sergei would kiss and hug and touch, reassuring one another of their love and teamwork. But now was not the time to mourn Sergei, Ekaterina reminded herself, but simply to celebrate him as someone who had loved life.

Sergei Grinkov had been the solid member of the pair, lifting his slender and graceful companion high into the air and throwing her into beautiful, soaring twists, always ready to catch her when she returned to earth. Life imitated art off the ice as well. As Ekaterina Gordeeva's husband, Sergei cared for her, making life seem idyllic for his "Katia," as he and their friends called her. "He was calmer than me," Ekaterina recalls. "I was more nervous. He was stable."

Friends and skating fans did not know which was more perfect, their skating or their love. All agreed that Gordeeva and Grinkov, or G & G, as they were affectionately dubbed, might be the best pairs skaters in history. Their passion for skating had culminated in four world championship titles and two Olympic gold medals, and their passion for each other led to their proudest achievement, a beautiful daughter named Daria. Life for the family seemed charmed—they were young, successful, and happy. But in one swift moment, it was all gone.

On November 20, 1995, Gordeeva and Grinkov were in Lake Placid, New York, practicing for the opening of the traveling show Discover Card Stars on Ice. The pair had started touring with the ice show in 1991, the year they were married. Stars on Ice features many of the top names in professional skating, including Scott Hamilton, Kristi Yamaguchi, and Paul Wylie. That morning, Ekaterina and Sergei were happy to be working on a new program with choreographer Marina Zueva. Sergei's back, which had been plaguing him off and on for over four years, was not giving him any problems as they practiced the elements of this program, a story set to the music of Edvard Grieg's Piano Concerto in A Minor. In the program, Ekaterina portrayed a weakened person whom Sergei rejuvenates, giving her energy and life. The program had special meaning for Ekaterina because she believed that it reflected Sergei's influence in her life. They worked on adding a double flip to the program and had decided on a beautiful closing pose just the afternoon before. Anxious to run through the program before Marina flew back to Canada, the pair warmed up and took the ice. The music washed over the rink as they glided through the opening and, as usual, made no mistakes.

Then Sergei missed a lift. Gordeeva, surprised not to feel her husband's strong hands about her waist, turned to him. "Is it your back?" she asked. As Sergei shook his head "no," he hit the boards separating the ice rink from the stands and grasped for something to hold himself up. He then crumpled to the ice. "What's wrong, Serioque?" Ekaterina asked, using a term of endearment that she saved for tender moments with her husband. "What's the matter?" There was no reply. Marina stopped the music, told Ekaterina to call 911, and began performing CPR on Sergei, who was not breathing. Because they had separated themselves from the other Stars on Ice skaters, who were practicing a group number on the larger, adjoining rink, Gordeeva ran for help. She was shaken and crying, but she tried to tell herself that everything would be all right. Sergei was only 28 years old, and he appeared to be the picture of health, muscular and strong. "I really thought he would be fine. I didn't even let myself think for a minute that he might die," Gordeeva wrote in her 1996 book *My Sergei: A Love Story.*

But when she returned with the others, the medical crew from the rink was working to revive him. Sergei had turned blue from a lack of oxygen. When the emergency medical technicians arrived, they used a defibrillator, a machine that delivers an electric shock to the heart to make it resume beating. Paramedics tried this technique three times on the ice and twice more in the parking lot before the ambulance, with Ekaterina in the front seat, rushed to nearby Adirondack Medical Center in Saranac Lake, New York. But it was too late. Sergei had died on the ice of a massive heart attack. Ekaterina and three-year-old Daria were now alone.

"He didn't look dead. It looked like he was just sleeping," Ekaterina later recalled. "Even one eye was open a little bit, and the whole time I thought maybe he was looking at

Friends carry Sergei Grinkov's coffin to the Vagankovsky Cemetery in Moscow on November 25, 1995, accompanied by a Russian military honor guard. The popular skater's unexpected death from a heart attack stunned the skating world.

me. He even looked like he was breathing. His hands were cold, but when I felt his shoulders and chest, they were still warm." Ekaterina tried to warm his hands, but it did no good. It was then that Katia realized she would never again feel the tender warmth of Sergei's touch. Stunned, she unlaced the skates that he would never wear again.

Doctors later found that Sergei, like an estimated 20 percent of the world's population, carried a defective heart gene that may cause blood clots and contribute to heart attacks. Dr. Francis Varga, who performed the autopsy on Sergei, said, "The entire front half of his heart muscle and a part of the left side of his heart muscle were deprived of oxygen. . . . If he continued [skating] at all on any schedule, it was only a question of time. . . . Unless his condition was discovered and he had a bypass, the probability of survival for him was remote. Many times in young people the first sign of coronary artery disease is sudden death."

Doctors also discovered that Sergei had suffered a very mild heart attack the day before his death, but the skater had most likely attributed whatever pain he may have felt to his persistent back injuries. One doctor's final discovery provided some relief for those close to Sergei. Dr. Josh Schwartzberg reported, "He was dead the moment he hit the ice—he felt no pain." And "the last thing Sergei [saw]," skater and friend Rosalynn Sumners said, "was Katia in her landing position, which is everything they had worked for since they were children in Moscow."

Sergei's death stunned the skating world, which mourned along with his young and seemingly fragile widow. Ekaterina had the support of her skating friends, Marina Zueva, her family, and countless others, and she found the courage to continue her life. It was not easy; in fact, for days after Sergei's death Katia just wanted to sleep, wondering why she had to be awake when almost everything she had lived for was gone. But there were things that had to be done. Even if her heart and mind were elsewhere, she had to say good-bye to Sergei again.

Three months after Sergei Grinkov's death, the skating world, including the cast of Stars on Ice and Ekaterina herself, gathered at the Hartford Civic Center in tribute to the man who had touched so many lives. They called it "A Celebration of a Life." So many skaters had asked to skate in the tribute that some had to be turned down.

The arena was completely filled with a crowd that was there to remember Sergei. The fans' enthusiasm was electric and affected all of the evening's performances, making each skater's routine seem more inspired than the last. With the crowd cheering and on its feet, the lights went up and Katia stood alone in a beautiful chiffon costume with a white bodice that turned into gray at the skirt. The costume was very similar to the one that she and Sergei had chosen for the new program they had never gotten to perform. Katia wore her hair back in a bun, and the sleeveless dress revealed her shoulders and arms. She

Katia hugs her daughter, Daria, after finishing her routine during the show "A Celebration of a Life."

seemed so small, but when the sweet strains of the Adagietto from Mahler's Fifth Symphony began to play, her graceful movements seemed to fill the ice.

The program was meant to depict Katia skating with Sergei for the last time. At the beginning, she pretended to hold his hand as she took the ice, seeming happy and content. In the middle of the routine, when he is taken from her, she shows anguish, asking God why this happened. The scene of Gordeeva on her knees on the ice, pretending to cry, brought tears to many people in the audience. She then rose and jubilantly skated for Sergei, thanking God for giving him to her, even if it was only for a short time. As the program ended, Katia stretched her arms up toward the sky, and moved across the ice on her toes, using her toe picks, the small, sharp ridges on the front of a skate blade. She appeared to be sending a hug up to Heaven, as if to tell Sergei that this night and performance were dedicated to him.

Strength and power were all that Katia felt on the ice, for she sensed Sergei's presence with her. "Just trust Sergei, and he will help you," Marina had told Gordeeva before her tribute program. And Ekaterina knew that he was there. When she finished the program, she began to cry. She skated over to Daria and picked her up, circling the ice as they hugged each other. The tiny towhead put her head on Katia's shoulder and patted her mother's back.

The finale of the night featured Gordeeva and all of the evening's other skaters. They paired up and each recreated a pose from various Gordeeva and Grinkov programs over the years. Katia skated through them and then skated to the music of a Russian folk dance. As the night came to a close, Ekaterina took the microphone and addressed the applauding crowd:

> I'm so happy this evening happened, and I'm sad it's all over. I want to start it over again. I want to thank all of you, because I know I will not be able to skate here if you did not come tonight. I'm so happy I was able to show you my skating. But I want you to know that I skated today not alone. I skated with Sergei. It's why I was so good. It wasn't me. . . . I don't have enough words, but I also want to wish to all of you: Try to find happiness in every day. And say just one extra time that you love the person who lives with you. Just say "I love you."

Ekaterina Gordeeva and Sergei Grinkov glide across the ice in unison during the 1986 World Championships. Both started skating at an early age: Katia was four years old when she first stepped onto the ice at the Central Red Army Club.

2

THE TINY SKATER
AND HER PARTNER

KATIA WAS BORN Ekaterina Alexandrovna Gordeeva on May 28, 1971, in Moscow, the capital of the Union of Soviet Socialist Republics (U.S.S.R.). Katia's father, Alexander Alexeyevich Gordeev, had met 14-year-old Elena Levovna at a dance class in 1965. They married in 1970, when Elena was 19, and Katia was born the following year. In 1975, Katia's little sister Maria Alexandrovna Gordeeva was born.

Russians do not have middle names. Instead, they are given a birth name, followed by variations of their father's first and last names. Ekaterina is equivalent to Katherine in English, while Alexandrovna is Katia's father's name with a special feminine ending, and Katia's last name is the feminine variation of her father's, Gordeev. Twenty-one years later, when the skater's daughter Daria was born, she became Daria Sergeyevna Grinkova.

Sisters Katia and Maria had the good fortune to be born into a happy family. Katia's father was a folk dancer who toured the world with the famous Moiseev dance company. Ekaterina inherited her father's grace and athletic ability. Alexander was a loving and devoted father with high expectations for his daughters. His dream was for Ekaterina to be a ballet dancer. Katia's mother was a teletype operator for Tass, the Soviet news agency. Because she also traveled for her work, Katia and Maria were often left in the care of their maternal grandmother, whom they lovingly called *babushka*. The arrangement was convenient because the entire family, along with Elena's father, Lev Faloseev, whom they called *diaka*, shared a five-room apartment in Moscow. Faloseev, who had been a colonel in a tank division during World War II, worked for the military and taught tank warfare at the Red Army academy. Because of his important military position, the family was able to live comfortably during a time when many in the Soviet Union were struggling. Members of the military who were deemed essential to the Soviet Union were often given special places to live and privileges not offered to others.

Katia grew up happy and loved. From the balcony of their apartment, she could see the Moscow River, soldiers on parade marching on their way to Red Square, and holiday fireworks. She even witnessed the passing of the Olympic torch on her street in 1980. While she did not yet dream of being an Olympic champion, the prospect of becoming anything she wanted was not inconceivable to nine-year-old Katia. She was sheltered from the outside world. She did not know about government, politics, or the tumultuous times in her country.

The U.S.S.R., one of the world's two "superpowers" from 1945 until 1991, was governed under a political ideology known as Communism. Under this system, a central bureaucracy regulated nearly every aspect of people's lives in the Soviet Union. Russians did not own property; instead, all was distributed by the state. The government also controlled the amount of food that was grown by Russian farmers, and owned all factories and outlets for production of consumer goods, such as cars, washing machines, or refrigerators. The ultimate goal of

this system, a variation on socialism that had been proposed by economist/philosopher Karl Marx in the 19th century, was a society in which the state provides for the needs of all its citizens equally.

Following World War II, the Soviet Union attempted to spread its Communist ideology throughout the world. To this end, the U.S.S.R. installed puppet governments, whose decisions were directed by the Soviets, in most of the nations of Eastern Europe—Poland, Hungary, Czechoslovakia, Bulgaria, Romania, and the eastern half of Germany. It also supported pro-Soviet rebel groups in

A night view of Moscow showing Red Square. Alexander and Elena Gordeev raised Katia and her younger sister, Maria, in the U.S.S.R.'s capital city.

their efforts to take over the governments of Third World countries around the world. As a result, the U.S.S.R.'s relations with the world's other superpower, the United States, were strained and sometimes hostile during this period, known as the Cold War.

Although the Soviet Union was an exceptional military power, with enough nuclear weapons to destroy the world, for most of its people life was a far cry from the Communist ideal that Marx had espoused. In fact, for many life was not much different than for those in a poverty-stricken Third World country. There was a housing shortage, lack of quality goods to buy, and too little fresh food on market shelves. The Communist government was corrupt and oppressive. Industrial production was slow, and goods were often poorly made or did not work at all. Katia would see a lot change in her country while she was growing up.

But despite the internal problems of the Soviet Union, its national athletic program played a large role in Ekaterina's skating career. Soviet athletes were not only highly successful and skilled, but also revered in their society. Those who achieved greatness were rewarded with money, homes, cars, and national respect. If a child showed promise in a sport, he or she was sent to elaborate training facilities. If athletes won an inter- national competition, they were expected to make their sport a career.

Katia's family was not thinking of skating as a career when four-year-old Katia first stepped onto the ice. They were merely interested in a physical activity for their young daughter. In the summer of 1975, on vacation at the Black Sea, Katia's parents met a skater who trained at the Central Red Army Club (called CSKA), the most prestigious sports club in the country. The minimum age to be considered for admittance to the club was five years old, so this newfound friend told officials at the club that Katia was five, even though she was only four.

That September, Katia tried out and was accepted. She was so small that even the smallest skates manufactured in the U.S.S.R. were several sizes too large for her. Katia's mother and grandmother knitted several pairs of socks so that her feet would not fall out of the skates.

At first, Katia just saw skating as a fun activity. "If it hadn't been skating, it would have been gymnastics or dance," she admitted later. But while Katia was enjoying herself on the ice, the coaches at the club had bigger plans in mind for their tiny skater. They knew how to train a young child for future success. Katia was an ideal skater: small (a plus in women's figure skating), lean, strong, and exceptionally disciplined. She used to wake her parents up early in the morning to drive her to practice. "I can't miss it. It's my job," she would insist. In her first year, Ekaterina skated twice a week, and by age five her training had doubled to four times a week.

When she was seven, Katia, considered a promising athlete, was told to attend sports school at CSKA. Here, students took regular classes in addition to training for their respective sport. After classes, Katia headed to the Central Red Army Club's ice rink for practice. Standards were strict at CSKA; if students did not show sufficient improvement in their sport, they were not promoted to the next grade in the sports school. When Katia was seven, there were 40 students in her CSKA class. But by the time she graduated 11 years later, there were only 10. Katia was never at the very top of her class. Her jumps were not as strong as they would have to be to succeed as a singles skater, but her coach told her that she would have a successful future as a pairs skater. The club's rules stated, however, that Katia must wait until she was 11 years old to be matched with a partner.

Until she was 10 years old, summers were free time. From June until September the family visited their *dacha*, or summer home, which was located an hour north of Moscow. The dacha was near both a forest and a river. Katia would play with Maria, creating plays and dancing, painting and coloring, building huts, and fishing. But Katia's favorite summertime activity was picking mushrooms with her grandfather. The two would awaken very early and spend all day outside finding the best mushrooms in the forest. Then they would bring them home to cook. These times were very dear to Katia, and she would remember them as she was required to spend more and more time practicing on the ice.

In the spring of 1982 Ekaterina turned 11, and she and her friend, Oksana Koval, were told to visit the large ice rink where the pairs and male skaters practiced. Both were being considered as partners for 15-year-old Sergei Grinkov. But that summer, Oksana left skating and joined ballet school. At the insistence of her father, Katia also auditioned at the ballet school, but she purposely did poorly so that she could continue skating. When she learned that she had been chosen to skate with Sergei, Gordeeva was very excited. Sergei was handsome, stylish, and—most important—a good skater. At first, Grinkov was unsure about the match and nervous about skating with a partner. Like Katia, his jumps were not as strong as they needed to be to continue as a singles skater. He was worried about the lifts that are required in pairs skating, but after he started upper-body conditioning, lifts were never a problem.

Sergei had a different temperament from his young partner, and had grown up in a different environment. He was born Sergei Mikhailovich Grinkov on February 4, 1967, in Moscow. His parents, Anna Filipovna and Mikhail Kondrateyevich, both worked for the Moscow police department. But they lived in the city of Lipetsk, nearly eight hours away from Moscow by train. With no one at home to care for Sergei, his parents would drop him off at day care on Monday morning and not return until after work on Friday! When Sergei was older, his parents moved to an apartment on the outskirts of Moscow. Although Sergei's sister, Natalia, was seven years older than Sergei, the two were very close growing up.

Whereas Katia was good at following rules and did what she was told, Sergei was a nonconformist who liked to do his own thing. In future years, he sometimes complained about the hypocrisy of the parties held after competitions or ice shows, where corporate sponsors whispered praise to almost every skater in the room in hopes of striking a business deal. Katia believed that Sergei would rather have spent an evening with skating fans than with celebrities, or even the other skaters. Ekaterina was drawn to Sergei's charm right from the start and she envied his free-spirited ways. She hoped that even though he was so much older, one day they might be friends.

Everything that Katia and Sergei had learned as singles skaters had to be relearned when they skated as a pair. They had to align their bodies and skate in unison. Because Sergei was so much taller than Katia, he was forced to skate using smaller strides. Fortunately, they had a patient coach named Vladimir Zaharov.

Spirals, jumps, lifts, and throws are pairs skating's essential elements, and the new partners had to master them. From the start, Ekaterina felt safe in Sergei's arms during lifts, but the throws terrified her. She fell repeatedly trying to learn how to land. But Sergei was patient and never lost his temper. Meanwhile, Katia saw that some of the other men who skated with a partner yelled at their female counterparts or threw their partners in an unexpected direction just to be cruel. She was thankful to have someone like Sergei to rely on. And with patience and practice, Katia eventually landed the throws.

In 1982, when Katia turned 11, she learned that she would begin skating with a partner— a 15-year-old named Sergei Grinkov who was handsome, stylish, and a good skater.

The first year as a pair passed quickly for Gordeeva and Grinkov. Katia was serious about skating, just as she was about everything else. Her quiet personality and hobby of needlepointing earned Katia the nickname *BabaKatia*, which means "little grandmother." While the other skaters teased her for her habits, Sergei did not, especially when Katia's grandmother would pack her cookies and snacks. Others found her large bag, packed with food, needles and thread, and every possible item that a skater might need, humorous, but Sergei loved the food. Babushka would make Sergei *pirochkis*, small pastries stuffed with meat and cheese, and tell Katia to give him the other treats. "If you don't want to eat it, Sergei will have it." Later, when they were with Stars on Ice, skater Brian Orser remembered: "Quite often when we were on tour, when you wanted to go out to dinner, they were the first to call. He didn't like turkey, but he liked sushi, and so did Katia. He'd eat his, and finish hers, too." Sergei was also a fan of the catering at the many rinks the ice tour visited. "Ready for free food, Sergei?" Scott Hamilton would ask. "Ab-so-LUTE-ly!!" Sergei would reply.

Sergei was a typical boy who enjoyed many things—all kinds of sports, sleeping, and hanging out with friends. These other interests almost put an early end to his pairs skating career. In their second year skating together, Sergei was 16 and not totally committed to the discipline of twice-a-day practices that his sport required. He missed a morning practice and Coach Zaharov lost his patience. "You don't have a future with Sergei, and I'm not going to coach him anymore," Zaharov told Katia. "You, Katia, will keep skating as a singles skater and we'll look for another partner for you."

But Katia knew that her future in skating was as Sergei's partner. "I'm not sure why, but I always believed Sergei was the only one who could skate with me," Katia admitted later. "It had nothing to do with having romantic feelings toward him. I thought that he was a very attractive man, but since I was so little, and he was so much older, I never though that he'd have special feelings for me." After Katia and Sergei's parents met with Zaharov, they decided to let the pair decide for themselves. "It was then that Sergei and I made the commitment to skate together, to become a team," Gordeeva recalls in *My Sergei*. Instead of Sergei, it was Zaharov who left the pair. Katia and Sergei's new coach, Nadezheda Shevalovskaya, asked a friend to create skating programs for her new pair. Marina Zueva, who at the time was studying for a degree in choreography, became an important part of both the personal and skating lives of Katia and Sergei.

In December 1983, just three months after changing coaches, Gordeeva and Grinkov entered their first Junior World Championships in Sapporo, Japan, and finished fifth. Katia was very nervous, and they both made some mistakes. Even though the performance was not their best, she remembered just feeling happy that it was over and knew that it would be easier next time. "This first competition in Japan was a big adventure for us. It [felt] like a vacation with my older brother."

After another year of training, competing, and getting used to being a pair, during which they again switched to a new coach, Stanislav Leonovich, Katia and Sergei were eager to show the progress they had made. In 1984, the Junior World Championships were held in the mountains of Colorado Springs, Colorado. The altitude affected many of the skaters' performances, but not Gordeeva and Grinkov's. Although they were not favored to medal, the pair won the competition—their first major victory. Their commitment to stay together had begun to pay off.

For 13-year-old Gordeeva and 17-year-old Grinkov, their first visit to the United States was almost as

To succeed, Katia and Sergei had to learn how to skate as a team. Despite months of practice that sometimes became frustrating, the skaters remained committed to helping each other develop. "I'm not sure why," Katia later commented, "but I always believed Sergei was the only one who could skate with me."

memorable as their win. "It was like a little fairy tale. It was Christmas and there was a lot of snow, and Christmas trees decorated with beautiful ornaments," Katia later recalled in *My Sergei*. Although they didn't have much money, the two had fun buying gifts and exchanging Russian goods with shopkeepers for American souvenirs to give friends and family. Because there was a shortage of children's clothes and other necessities in Russia, Gordeeva took the opportunity to buy things for herself and her younger sister.

Shortly after their victory, back home in Moscow,

Sergei turned 18. Katia gave him the first of many gifts she would give him as the two became friends—a key chain with a little cap gun. Katia's father had bought the novelty for her as a token from a trip to Spain, but she had set it aside as a gift for Sergei. "I thought it was very cool, and since I'm [a] girl, I [didn't] need this. . . . I thought he would like it and he kept this chain," Gordeeva recalled. Around this time, Ekaterina's feelings for Sergei began to change. She liked being with him off the ice and found him attractive in a new way. These feelings were "something very new and different" to the 13-year-old girl. Unfortunately, she had no girlfriends her own age to confide in. Katia's youngest female friend was a 20-year-old skater, past the age of giggles and crushes on boys that most young teenage girls experience, and Maria was only nine and did not like boys yet.

In May 1985 Katia turned 14, and although she invited Sergei to her party, he phoned her and asked if they could meet so he could give her a birthday gift. Nervous and excited, Katia ran to their designated meeting place, the subway station, to find Sergei holding a huge white and brown stuffed dog. She kept the precious gift on her bed, sleeping with the stuffed animal when she was at home in Moscow.

As the pair got to know one another better, their skating grew stronger. This blossoming friendship would help them through a difficult time with a tough new coach.

In 1986, Gordeeva and Grinkov reached the pinnacle of their sport, winning the World Championships in Geneva, Switzerland.

3

BECOMING ONE

UNDER THE INSTRUCTION of Leonovich and Zueva, Gordeeva and Grinkov improved. For the 1985–86 season, Zueva created two new programs for the pair: a short program to thc piano ragtime music of Henry Lodge and a challenging long program to a medley of big band music by musicians such as Glenn Miller and Duke Ellington. The programs included difficult jumps, challenged the duo's acting skills, and involved some fancy footwork. At the start of the competitive season, Sergei and Katia were still working out the kinks in these programs and trying to master one of the harder jumps, the side-by-side triple salchow. This jump requires the skater to take off from a back inside edge of one blade and complete three revolutions before landing on the back outside edge of the other skate. Unfortunately, Sergei fell on the jump at the Skate Canada competition and Stanislav Zhuk, the head coach of the army club, witnessed the error.

After the pair's disastrous showing at the 1985 *Moscow News* competition, their coaching became a serious issue. Because he was the club's leader, Zhuk was in a position to oversee the training of all athletes and make decisions about their future. A former pairs skater himself, Zhuk took Gordeeva and Grinkov from Leonovich and declared that he would coach them himself. Although this was a sign that they showed promise, the coaching change turned out to be a curse for the pair.

Zhuk enjoyed and abused his position of authority. He drank, spoke dirty to the boys, and liked to flirt with the older female skaters. (Because she had not yet matured, he never bothered Katia, however.) Zhuk's training was different from anything Gordeeva and Grinkov had yet experienced. He did not like choreography in programs and focused instead on element after element with nothing in between. He also thought it best to separate Katia and Sergei off the ice so that they would only concentrate on their conditioning.

While Katia disliked Zhuk, she never spoke back to their coach or gave him reason to reprimand her. Sergei, on the other hand, was more outspoken. He had finished high school, and he believed that he should be permitted to spend time off the ice as he wished. "After practice, what I do is none of your business," Sergei would tell Zhuk. "If I want a beer, I'll have one. If it's Saturday and we don't skate, I won't get up at 7:00 A.M." Gordeeva later wrote that her partner "had his own code for living. Even though he never told anybody his code, he always lived by it. Sergei knew what was right and what wasn't. I knew only what I was told."

Hard training was essential to Zhuk's coaching method. When they were not on the ice, Katia and Sergei did off-ice conditioning—running stairs, weight training, and undersea diving, which Zhuk believed helped their breathing. Their schedule began early in the morning and lasted until evening. Although they came in second in the 1986 U.S.S.R. Nationals, Katia believed

they were overtrained and their program was too mechanical. By the World Championships that year, held in Geneva, Switzerland, Katia and Sergei were physically tired, but they were especially tired of Zhuk. Although they won the competition with a clean program, they felt no glory on the medal stand. "I was very, very happy that the competition was over," Katia remembered. "And when I came back to the room, I started crying because I was very disappointed because I thought, this is [the] World Championships. You have this gold medal and you're not happy."

As a pairs skater in the 1950s, Stanislav Zhuk was a champion. However, although the Soviet skaters that he coached 20 years later were often successful, many people disagreed with his training methods and his refusal to incorporate artistic choreography into his skaters' programs.

After the win they went on a 20-city tour sponsored
by the International Skating Union (ISU). The other
skaters enjoyed traveling, but under Zhuk's watchful
eye Katia and Sergei were not allowed to have any fun.
One day on the tour, Grinkov went for a walk with
fellow Russian skater Alexander Fadeev and American
champion Brian Boitano. Boitano asked Fadeev, who
spoke English, to ask Sergei what he loved about skating. "Sergei said that he didn't love skating. He skated
because he had to," Katia remembered. What had started
out as fun had turned into unpleasant work for both
Gordeeva and Grinkov. While they were well-trained and
disciplined skaters, their hearts and souls were not in
the sport. Katia thought Zhuk made her tough and more
confident, but she knew there was more bad than good in
his coaching.

The pair knew that in order to stay in the sport and
progress they needed a new coach. Others felt the same
way—Zhuk's behavior had become even more abusive. In
the summer of 1986, while they were preparing for the new
season, Grinkov, Fadeev, fellow skater Anna Kondrashova,
and Zueva drafted a letter to CSKA officials asking that
Zhuk be removed as head coach. At their insistence, Katia
signed the letter as well, not knowing what would come
of their request.

Katia's parents were skeptical about dismissing
Zhuk, because under his coaching Grinkov and
Gordeeva had won the world championship. Their atti-
tude toward Zhuk changed, however, after they saw
that the pair were not prepared for the Skate Canada
competition in the fall of 1986. Then, when Zhuk
promised Gordeeva some much-needed vacation time,
her parents scheduled a trip to the *dacha*. But on the
day they were to leave for the country, Zhuk made
Katia listen to music for a new program for the entire

day. The Gordeevs witnessed Zhuk's broken promise bring their daughter to tears, and her father said, "That's enough."

With pressure from the skaters and their parents, Russian officials again appointed Leonovich to coach Gordeeva and Grinkov. Zhuk was allowed to keep his title at the club, but he would no longer be in charge of the pair. With Leonovich as coach, skating became fun again. Marina Zueva helped create innovative programs. "Marina, Leonovich, Sergei, and I used to be the envy of all the other skaters because we had such a good rapport on the ice, always laughing and enjoying ourselves," Katia recalled in *My Sergei*. Ironically, with the more lighthearted mood, Sergei began taking the sport more seriously, and Katia and Sergei felt more unified, more like a pair than ever before. This new commitment showed in their skating as they won the 1987 Soviet Nationals.

Preparing for the European Championships that year, they added a split quadruple twist lift to their program. They were one of the few pairs to ever perform this extremely difficult element. As they took the ice at the Europeans in Sarajevo, Yugoslavia, they felt ready. But despite their exuberance and preparation, Leonovich's relative inexperience as a coach would cause a problem in this competition. One minute into their long program, the elastic strap on Sergei's pant leg broke and the referee blew his whistle, signaling the pair to stop skating. Sergei and Katia looked to Leonovich for guidance, but he made no sign for them to stop. Determined to finish what up until that point had been a clean, well-skated program, they continued. Their music stopped, but the crowd cheered them on. Afterward, Gordeeva and Grinkov were exhausted and very confused.

Leonovich had not known that his skaters' great effort

Skating became fun again for Sergei and Ekaterina when Zhuk was replaced as coach by Stanislav Leonovich and Marina Zueva was reinstated as the pair's choreographer.

would not count because the referee had stopped the routine. In order to be given their marks, the pair would have to skate again or be disqualified. Katia and Sergei, believing that they had skated their best, did not want to skate again, and their coach did not push them. They were out of the competition.

The disappointed team prepared for the 1987 World Championships in Cincinnati, Ohio, with new energy. They skated the same program, this time with no surprises and no mistakes, and repeated as world champions. "This was the competition that I was feeling that 'I'm with Sergei and I'm with Stanislav and Marina is watching us.' I was feeling like a group. I was just very, very proud of all of us, not of me, actually, but all of us—feeling like we [were] a team," Katia later said, indicating that she felt the performance at the 1987 Worlds may have been the best they ever skated in competition.

The beautiful skating and easy chemistry of Gordeeva and Grinkov caught the eye of skating promoter and tour organizer Tom Collins. Looking for a pairs team to round out his collection of singles skaters and ice dancers, Collins asked Katia and Sergei to go on a month-long tour of 25 cities in the United States. The pair was excited at the opportunity, and they grew even closer on the tour. Although Katia would one day learn to speak English, neither she nor Sergei were able to communicate well with the other skaters or with their new legions of American fans. Although it often made the pair self-conscious, the language barrier did not matter on the ice. The skating of Gordeeva and Grinkov did not need words to convey its meaning.

The tour also changed Katia and Sergei's relationship. The two talked, sat together on the bus, and went to dinner together. Others noticed the blossoming affection between them. One day in particular, it became evident to Katia that Sergei cared for her as more than a skating partner. On a rare day off, the two went to

*After a disappointing disquali-
fication at the 1987 European
Nationals, Katia and Sergei
performed the same routine
flawlessly to defend their
World Championship title
in '87.*

Disneyland with married friends Sergei Ponomarenko
and Marina Klimova. Sergei bought Katia ice cream,
put his arm around her in line for rides, hugged her, and
held her hand. "It was [a] great feeling. . . . It was
something new and exciting." Katia hoped that the newfound intimacy they shared would not change when
they returned to Moscow and their old way of life.

Refreshed and energized by this reprieve from competition, the pair began preparing for the 1988 Winter
Olympic Games. They began training in June 1987 at a
training facility in Soviet Georgia. Here, Marina introduced them to their two new Olympic programs. The
short program was to "The March of the Toreadors"
from the opera *Carmen*, and the long program was a
medley of piano pieces by Mendelssohn, Chopin, and

Mozart. The costumes, sky blue with white flowers on the shoulder, reflected the fresh choreography and springtime feel of the program. Katia liked it right away. She was also getting excited about the Olympics and enjoying the preparation. "We'd begin each day with a morning workout before breakfast. We ran and lifted before lunch. In the afternoon we worked with Marina. Then we had another workout at 5 P.M., before dinner." But the hours Gordeeva looked forward to most were the evenings when she and her partner could spend quiet time together. They often spent their free time hiking or picnicking.

Because they were busy practicing, Gordeeva and Grinkov did not participate in many of the competitions leading up to the Olympics. However, they did participate in, and win, the *Moscow News* competition. While they were training for the Olympics, Sergei accidentally dropped his partner during practice. He hit a soft rut in the ice and Katia, who was in a star lift with her arms and legs fully extended high in the air above Sergei's head, fell to the ice forehead first. She suffered a severe concussion and was hospitalized for six days. "I lay there worrying about missing practice and the Olympics, and I was mad at Sergei because I thought the fall was his mistake. Then there was a knock at the door, and it was Sergei. He was carrying a dozen roses, and he was very, very upset," Gordeeva later recalled. Sergei visited his partner three more times before she was released from the hospital, and he visited every day that she was required to rest at home.

Two weeks after the fall, Katia and Sergei were back on the ice. "He wanted to express his feeling[s] to me, I think, somehow, and the only way it would be possible would be on the ice," Gordeeva wrote in *My Sergei*. "He was holding me so tight now. I thought he was never going to let me go. . . . Something changed in him and in our skating." Sergei never dropped Katia again.

Katia's parents suggested that she ask Grinkov to celebrate the New Year with them that year. Perhaps they suspected that Katia and Sergei were becoming more than skating partners. After witnessing Sergei's attention to Katia after her fall, they knew he cared for her very deeply. Katia did not know if Sergei would say yes to her invitation, let alone spend the entire night with her family. She was excited when he accepted.

December 31 is an important holiday for Russian families. In the Soviet Union, Christmas was not celebrated because religion was banned, so many Russian families turned New Year's Eve into a children's holiday, complete with many traditional Christmas items—a lighted tree, presents, and the Russian Santa Claus, Grandfather Frost.

That year, the Gordeevas had a beautiful decorated tree, a feast of meat and fruits, and a bag of presents, dubbed in years past the "Santa Claus bag." After a midnight champagne toast, the group opened presents. Katia gave Sergei a needlepoint picture of a clown that she had worked on nearly all year. New Year's Eve 1988 was also the introduction of a new tradition. At exactly midnight, Elena broke an old plate on the floor and everyone was supposed to take a piece of the plate, hide it, and make a wish. Katia wished that she would skate well in the Olympics. She never asked Sergei about his wish.

The 1988 European Championships were held in Prague. Katia and Sergei did not skate their best, but they still won the competition. With this victory, the biggest competition of their career—the Olympic Games—was upon them. The legacy of Soviet skaters loomed over Gordeeva and Grinkov. Since 1964 the

Soviet Union had won the gold medal in the pairs event at every Olympics, and the U.S.S.R. expected nothing less than gold from Katia and Sergei. A lot of pressure was on the shoulders of the young skaters.

On January 27, 1988, Sergei and Katia left for Calgary, Canada, and the Winter Olympics. Katia's New Year's wish was about to come true.

Ekaterina Gordeeva and Sergei Grinkov show off their costumes for the 1988 Winter Olympic Games. There was intense pressure on the pair to win the Olympics, because they had won back-to-back World Championships and because Soviet skaters had dominated the pairs event, winning every Olympic competition since 1964.

4

A YEAR OF FIRSTS

NOT LONG AFTER they arrived in Calgary, Sergei turned 21. He had always worn a gold chain around his neck with a horseshoe charm for good luck, so Katia decided to give her partner the Calgary Olympic symbol charm to add to this chain. She didn't mind the other skaters teasing her about the gift and the feelings they suspected she had for him, because Sergei proudly wore the charm. On February 9, a day after moving into the Olympic village, Sergei got a bad stomach flu and was unable to practice for three days. Even after he recovered, Katia was incredibly homesick. The two lived on different floors and did not see each other very much, and Katia felt so much younger than the others. But the letters she received from her mother helped.

As the pairs skating competition opened, Katia went into their short program confident in her skating and relieved that the long wait was over. The program went smoothly, and the pair was in first place at the end of the round. The only problem they encountered was at the program's end, when the music stopped and they were not facing the judges. They quickly turned around and no one noticed the mistake. Another Russian pair, 1984 gold medalists Elena Valova and Oleg Vassiliev, was in second place, but Gordeeva and Grinkov were the favorites for the gold. A few nights later, they skated a flawless long program and lived up to both Soviet legacy and pre-Olympic predictions by winning the gold medal.

Sandra Bezic, a former Canadian pairs champion and choreographer who would eventually work with G & G, said of their Olympic performance, "It was heaven. He presented her so beautifully, like a cherished little sister. They are everything pairs skating should be." Sportswriter E. M. Swift agreed with Bezic about the beauty of their skating, saying it "tiptoed the line between athletics and art," but took a different view of the relationship between Gordeeva and Grinkov. "In this pair," he wrote, "there lies the tension of youth ready to blossom, of the older brother's friend, say, who suddenly realizes that the little girl with whom he is dancing has grown into a woman." Sportswriters, judges, and skating fans all over the world fell in love with Gordeeva and Grinkov. They watched, enchanted, as Katia spoke in her halting English, "Hello everybody, how are you?"

Surprisingly, nothing was organized to celebrate their Olympic victory. Sergei went out to celebrate with his friends, but Katia was too young to go to the nightclubs and bars they had planned to visit, so she decided to reward herself with an ice cream sundae from the soda fountain in the game room of the athletes' village. But to her disappointment, she found that the soda fountain had closed. After eating several bowls of plain ice cream in the cafeteria, she spent the most of the evening alone in her room, writing in her journal. "It's very weird that everything is all over," she wrote. "It all happened so quickly. We were so long preparing for this, then it all

Gordeeva and Grinkov swirl over the ice on the way to an Olympic gold medal in 1988.

happened in one second. . . . I really want to go home. I really miss my mom. Already, it's a little boring for me here."

The next 10 days were filled with interviews and photographs. It seemed like Sergei and Katia were always surrounded by the media or their fans. They held their first press conference, where Gordeeva was asked if, because of the four-year age difference, she thought one day Grinkov would be too old to skate with her. "I have never answered such a question," she told reporters. "But I don't think I will need another partner. I am used to him." When Sergei was asked about the pair's future, he said, "We will skate as long as we're still young."

During their first Olympics, Sergei made many new friends, but Katia felt shy and uncomfortable being the focus of the world's attention. It wasn't until she returned home to her family that she celebrated her gold medal performance. Just as he had done with all her other medals, Katia's father put the Olympic medal in a glass goblet filled with champagne and passed it around for everyone to take a sip. Then the family, including Sergei, visited a friend who lived on the Volga River, two-and-a-half hours north of Moscow. For five days, Katia and Sergei went snowmobiling, talked, ate, took saunas, and rested, finally basking in the glow of their Olympic win.

But soon the pair returned to skating, training for the World Championships in Budapest, Hungary. Drained both physically and emotionally, this time it was Katia who came down with the flu. The pair lost to Olympic silver medalists Elena Valova and Oleg Vassiliev after Katia fell trying to land a triple salchow throw.

Disappointed in their first world championship loss in three years, Katia decided to buy herself a new outfit for the awards banquet. When she entered, in a miniskirt and blouse, everyone could see that the cute, wispy, little girl had grown into a graceful and beautiful young woman.

On the European tour following the Worlds, Katia grew confused about her relationship with Sergei. While on the one hand he had started to notice her, speaking to her as he did his friends and often seeking out her company, he still did not include her in many of his outings. When they were asked to go on the Tom Collins tour again, Katia decided that she needed a break from skating. Although her coach tried to convince her to go, Katia remained firm in her decision to return to Moscow. While Sergei also wanted Gordeeva to join the tour, he respected his partner's decision and did not try to change her mind.

Instead of touring, Katia accompanied her parents on a two-week vacation at the Black Sea. While there, she received an invitation to attend a banquet that Soviet Union President Mikhail Gorbachev was giving in honor of the president of the United States, Ronald Reagan. Katia met these powerful world figures and sat next to Gorbachev's wife Raisa. When she returned home, Katia was disappointed to find that she had missed a visit from Sergei while she had been away. He had left her flowers and perfume as a 17th birthday gift.

Around her birthday, Katia noticed that she was having mood swings and was starting to have trouble landing jumps. She had grown two inches, to 5'2", and now weighed 95 pounds. The changes were affecting both her mind and body. Frustrated with herself, she often got upset at practice. But Sergei would calm her down with his advice. "Don't put yourself down," he once said. "You're not a little kid. If you're disappointed in yourself, don't show it to people. You have to have enough strength to handle it." He helped her through this difficult time, and more than ever Katia found herself attracted to her handsome partner. Throughout the autumn, she tried to lose some of the weight she had put on as her body matured. In November 1988, perhaps due to her intense workouts and diet, Katia suffered a stress fracture in her right foot. With a cast on her foot for an entire month, she decided to use the time off the ice in order to improve her English.

Once the cast came off, Katia could not return to the ice right away but instead started lifting weights, swimming, and practicing lifts off the ice with Sergei. She went to the rink to watch him skate through the new program Marina had created for them. Sergei could not stand to see her upset at not being able to skate, so he lifted her off her feet and skated her around the ice. "It was better than being well," she remembered.

The New Year was approaching, and Katia invited Sergei to spend the holiday with her family at Yegor Guba's, whose home they had visited after their gold medal win earlier that year. But Sergei told her that he had already made plans with his friend Alexander "Sasha" Fadeev. When they arrived at Yegor's, Katia was disappointed that she would not be able to spend the New Year with Sergei. Instead of celebrating, she decided to take a nap. She was awakened by a slightly drunk Sergei, who had changed his mind about coming. On the way to the country, he and Sasha had drunk Katia's gift, a bottle of sweet liqueur, and Sergei was ready to ring in the new year with his partner. He invited Katia to come with them to see Sasha's new sauna, which was located not far from Yegor's home. Fadeev's sauna was like most Russian saunas—a three-room log cabin containing a dressing room, dining room, and the sauna room, which is heated by a wood-burning stove. When Fadeev opted for a sauna that night, he left Gordeeva and Grinkov alone in the eating area. They shared a drink, but she sensed that the usually calm Sergei seemed uncomfortable. "Then he said, 'Why don't we kiss?' Something like that. It wasn't really a question," Gordeeva wrote in *My Sergei*. "He gave me a gentle kiss on the mouth, and when he saw that I liked it, he gave me another one that was longer." Although Fadeev had suspected that the two had feelings for one another, he was still embarrassed when he emerged from the sauna for a drink to find Katia and Sergei kissing. Around nine o'clock in the evening, the three decided to return to Katia's family home for the festivities.

"After I left the sauna . . . I was a totally different person," Katia said. "I remember walking back and listening to the cold crunching of the snow beneath our footsteps. The fields were all blanketed in white, and the moon gave us shadows. It was so beautiful, and I was so happy." Katia did not tell anyone that night about the kisses she and Sergei had shared, or about the love they expressed for each other soon after. Although it had been a year of hard changes for Katia, 1988 had started with an Olympic gold medal and ended with the knowledge that Sergei loved her.

In early 1989, Katia and Sergei traveled to Birmingham, England, to watch the European Championships; they were unable to participate because they had missed valuable training time. There the two had a mini-vacation as a couple, going to pubs and spending time together.

Their blossoming relationship reminded Sergei of a promise that he had been made. The Soviet government had said that after the Olympics, Sergei would receive a car and his own apartment. Almost a year later, he had gotten neither. Upset that he was 22 years old and still

Katia and Sergei suffered a letdown after the Olympics, losing the 1988 World Championships, but they came back strong to recapture the title in 1989.

living at home, Sergei threatened to quit skating if he did not get what he was promised. He was given a car and told that he would soon get his own apartment. There was a housing shortage in Russia, and even married couples often had to live in their parents' apartments. Sergei's older sister had been forced to do this, and the strain had caused her marriage to end in divorce. Although he had not thought about marriage quite yet, Sergei wanted to have a place that he and Katia might one day call home.

The pair started practicing their routine for the World Championships in Paris, France. Their program, skated to the music of Johann Strauss Jr., was about a girl being asked to waltz at her first fancy ball. Although they had not skated competitively in months, they won their third world championship. "I just remember that it was probably the first time when I didn't pay too much attention in competition," Gordeeva later recalled. "I paid much more attention to Sergei."

In Paris, it was hard to hide their growing love, and many of the other skaters and coaches, including Marina Zueva, noticed the feelings between the two. They strolled around the city hand-in-hand, hugging and kissing, and dined together at sidewalk cafés. The two were sorry to have to say good-bye to Paris and dreamed of returning again.

Although Ekaterina Gordeeva and Sergei Grinkov had been partners on the ice for seven years, their blossoming relationship off the ice was something new and exciting for them both.

5

MARRIAGE AND MOTHERHOOD

AFTER ANOTHER EUROPEAN TOUR, Katia and Sergei decided to spend some time alone. Although they had known one another for nearly seven years and had worked closely as partners, their new relationship was different from anything either had ever known or expected. In mid-May of 1989, a few weeks before Katia's 18th birthday, the two traveled to Katia's family's new dacha and spent 10 days there relaxing together off the ice. Sergei had just gotten a new bull-terrier puppy he named Moshka. The two played with Moshka, and Katia cooked many of the meals that her babushka had taught her to make when she was a child.

When they returned from the country, Marina introduced them to their new program, a routine with music from Tchaikovsky's *Romeo and Juliet*. This program was the first in which Katia and Sergei were allowed creative input, and Sergei especially seemed to know where the different elements should fit. The program was incredibly popular with fans and judges, who also noticed the change in Gordeeva and Grinkov. The 1976 Olympic men's bronze medalist

Toller Cranston, now a choreographer, said of the *Romeo and Juliet* routine, "This was truly a performance. This was beauty and art wrought with athleticism. It's probably the most sophisticated piece they've ever done. . . . What it had was charm and beauty and an effortlessness that made it sublime."

Although beautiful, the program was deceptively difficult, especially for Sergei. Although Katia weighed only 95 pounds, Grinkov's years of throwing and lifting his partner had resulted in deep, recurring shoulder pain. Certain lifts and throws hurt him more than others, so wherever possible these moves were replaced. However, in the *Romeo and Juliet* routine Coach Leonovich had introduced a new lift that seemed to aggravate the injury. The loop lift was very beautiful, but very painful for Sergei. It required him to lift Katia with one arm.

At the 1990 European Championships in Leningrad, Katia and Sergei struggled with their short program. Katia missed a double axel, a difficult jump in which the skater takes off from a forward outside edge, performs two-and-a-half revolutions in the air, and lands on the back outside edge of the other foot. She also slipped during the death spiral. In this move the man plants his toe pick into the ice, and as he holds the hand of his partner, who is in an almost-horizontal layout position, he spins her around his feet so that her head almost touches the ice. Although it is beautiful and seemingly effortless when done correctly, the move requires just the right tilt to the man's body and very strong stomach muscles and courage from the woman. A mistake could mean a head injury or a very serious cut from her partner's blade.

Their mistakes were costly, but the pair was still in contention for a medal at the start of the long program after finishing in third place in the short program. The

beauty and difficulty of the *Romeo and Juliet* program won them the gold. Although the pair did not perform the number as well at the World Championships later that year in Halifax, Canada, they again won despite their mistakes.

Years of lifting and holding Ekaterina had injured Sergei Grinkov's shoulder, making difficult moves like the "death spiral" very painful.

In 1990, the pair won their fourth World Championship, skating one of their most beautiful programs to Tchaikovsky's Romeo and Juliet.

In the spring, Gordeeva and Grinkov decided to go on Tom Collins's tour again. It was a vacation from competing, and now that they were a pair off the ice as well as on it, the two went almost everywhere together. They enjoyed sightseeing on their days off, visiting cities such as New York, Los Angeles, and Philadelphia. However, when the tour was in Washington, D.C., Sergei received a phone call from Russia: his father had died of a heart attack. Sergei returned to Moscow for the funeral; he was morose and felt guilty for not having spent as much time with his father as he would have liked. Katia was also sorry that she had not gotten to know Sergei's father. They had only met on two occasions, but she had heard that in addition to physical similarities, Sergei's temperament and personality were just like Mikhail Grinkov's.

The tragedy strengthened Sergei's resolve that he and Katia should make a life together. "Some men are natural fathers, even before they are fathers, and Sergei was this kind of man," Katia said in her book *My Sergei*. Grinkov knew that in order to support a family, he would need to make more money than he and Katia did as amateurs. Gordeeva and Grinkov had been a couple for over a year. Their courtship was as natural and easy as their skating. The one thing holding Sergei back from marrying Katia was the apartment issue. "Before he got his apartment," Katia remembered, "we used to laugh that we would probably live in a car someday, set up house there and raise our children." Even after they were married, Katia's favorite place to be alone with Sergei was in the car, talking and driving. Sergei knew that as soon as he got his own apartment, he would ask Katia to marry him.

Perhaps Elena Gordeeva suspected Sergei's intentions, because around the time of Katia's 19th birthday, she suggested Katia be baptized in the Russian Orthodox faith so that she could be married in a church. Prior to the late 1980s, religion was banned in the Soviet Union and people were subject to persecution because of their religious beliefs. But following the reforms in the U.S.S.R. during that decade, religion was once again permitted in Russia. Katia was christened at the Church of Vladimir the Conqueror by Father Nikolai. She enjoyed learning about her new religion, and she also felt a special closeness to Father Nikolai. Although Katia had not grown up in a religious environment, she found the priest's beliefs both comfortable and inviting.

In the fall of 1990, Sergei finally received the title to a studio apartment in a Moscow high-rise building. It was on their first visit to the apartment that Sergei proposed. "It wasn't the way Americans propose to a woman," Katia explained. "He didn't give me a ring. He didn't get on his knees and ask me to marry him. Sergei just said, 'I would love for you to live with me in this apartment.'" The apartment was not suitable for living in yet, but Katia was overjoyed and imagined how it might look one day.

While they were planning the wedding, Katia and Sergei were also preparing to turn professional. "We started to talk more and more that maybe we were a little bit tired and we wanted to spend more time off the ice . . . and spend more time together. . . . We [were] also thinking that we [weren't] learning anything new, and we're kind of stuck. And it's why our skating is not getting better." Turning professional, both felt, was the solution to these problems. "We were very happy about it and we thought 'great' we have so much time now that we can learn new elements, we can heal Sergei's shoulder, we can go earn money as . . . professionals."

At the time, Katia's father was working for Tatiana Tarasova, a choreographer and coach who ran the Russian All-Stars tour. He urged Katia and Sergei to work with

Tatiana and join the tour. They agreed that it was time for a coaching change, but Marina Zueva refused to work with Tarasova because the two had many opposing styles. After much deliberation, Katia and Sergei chose Tarasova as their new coach, but they made no commitment to her tour. They were interested in working in America with more American skaters.

Without consulting any of their coaching staff or family, the two decided to sign a contract with International Management Group (IMG), and they prepared new programs for the World Professional Championships, held in Landover, Maryland, in December 1990. While many people were surprised by their decision, everyone close to them trusted that Grinkov and Gordeeva knew best.

At first, the young skaters were uncomfortable with all of the freedom they were allowed as professionals. For years, they had been told when to eat, what to practice on the ice, and how to train off the ice. Suddenly, all of these decisions were up to them. Although they did not win their early professional competitions, they were still generously paid for their performances.

At the beginning of 1991, Sergei decided he wanted to give his bride-to-be something special. In Germany, they went to an antique jewelry store and picked out an emerald ring with small diamonds in the setting. Katia vowed never to take off the ring. Then they applied for their marriage license and chose April 20th as the day to pick it up. In Russia, acquisition of a marriage license meant that the couple was officially married, but the two had decided to have a church wedding and banquet for their family and friends as well. On April 28, 1991, less than a year after he had baptized Katia, Father Nikolai married Ekaterina Gordeeva and Sergei Grinkov. Katia wore an off-white silk dress that she had bought in Toronto and flowers

Sergei and Katia beam after their first professional victory, at the 1991 World Professional Championships. The victory in December 1991 was their first as a married couple.

in her hair. Even though it rained on their wedding day, the banquet was lovely. The two danced their first waltz together (realizing that they had never danced together off the ice!) and enjoyed the company of family and friends.

As a wedding gift, Elena Gordeeva had overseen the renovation of Sergei's studio apartment. She cleaned and furnished the small space, leaving fresh flowers and a bottle of champagne for the newlyweds. "This apartment was the best gift she could have offered us: a new world for Seriozha and me," Katia later said.

Instead of going on a honeymoon, the pair decided to get back on the ice as quickly as possible. In February, still troubled by pain in his shoulder, Sergei had undergone surgery. During the procedure, the doctor discovered that Sergei's rotator cuff, the group of muscles that allows the rotation of the shoulder and arm, was torn, and another operation was needed. Just days before their wedding, Sergei had flown to the United States to see his doctor in Princeton, New Jersey, for the rotator-cuff surgery. This operation seemed to help. Hopeful, the pair joined the Tom Collins tour in mid-May and then went on the Russian All-Stars Tour to South Africa. This was almost like a honeymoon, as Katia and Sergei spent time together sightseeing and enjoying themselves.

The beauty of their skating had caught the eye of one of the most respected names in skating, choreographer Toller Cranston, who wanted to create a program for G & G. The two needed a technical program for the World Professional Figure Skating Championships, so they traveled to Toronto, Canada, to meet Cranston. The program he created, to the music of Tchaikovsky's *Nutcracker Suite*, was a perfect fit for the pair and they won the World Professional Championships that December. It was their first win in the professional arena.

Because they enjoyed the laid-back lifestyle of touring, Katia and Sergei joined the touring show Stars on Ice. Rehearsals began in Aspen, Colorado, in the fall of 1991. Other big skating names such as Scott Hamilton, Brian Orser, Debi Thomas, Rosalynn Sumners, and Kitty and Peter Carruthers were part of the tour. Although the language barrier presented problems for Katia and Sergei, everyone was very friendly to the new additions. While Katia spoke and understood limited English, Sergei knew practically none. Katia's command of the language began to improve around the American skaters, and Sergei also picked up phrases and expressions. Soon, Sergei had learned enough English to understand and laugh at Scott Hamilton's jokes and greet his fellow skaters. Kurt Browning was shocked one morning to hear Sergei speak English. "He was coming to the rink and saying 'Good morning, Kurt'," Browning recalled. "And I'd say, 'Oh hi, Sergei. I'm good. And you?' He'd always say, 'Oh, I'm not too bad.'"

While they were endearing themselves to their fellow skaters, for Katia the time was also difficult. That August, her babushka had died of cancer, and a friend, Canadian ice dancer Rob McCall, was dying of AIDS (Acquired Immune Deficiency Syndrome). "Rob died before the show opened," Katia remembered, "and when the tour got to Toronto, we did a benefit in his memory for a hospital specializing in AIDS research." Like Sergei, who grieved for both the recent loss of his father and the death of his best friend several years earlier in a car accident, Katia was learning to be strong during times of sorrow.

But their times with Stars on Ice were mostly fun. The tour bus was like a mini-home, stocked with food and drinks. They had fun relaxing, talking about their last performance, and looking forward to their next destination. When the tour went on break in late 1991, Gordeeva and

Grinkov were reluctant to return to Moscow. Instead, Katia and Sergei decided to stay in the United States.

After the Stars on Ice tour resumed, in January 1992 Katia began to feel strange. After visiting a doctor, she found out she was three weeks pregnant. "My first thought was, I don't want to have the baby," Katia admitted. "I was so young—twenty—and I was worried about missing a whole year of skating." She waited for the right time to tell her husband:

> I was very confused and undecided. . . . That night I still said nothing to Sergei. He was out late with some of his friends, which upset me, of course, and the next morning I was still angry with him. I felt sick, and somehow we got into a silly argument. I don't remember what it was about, but my hormones must have been making me crazy, because I blurted out: "I'm pregnant. I'm feeling bad, and you don't even care."

Sergei's reaction surprised Katia: he was excited. "We're going to have a baby," he kept saying proudly. Any doubts Katia had previously felt about having a baby were wiped away as soon as she saw her husband's reaction, and the two quickly adjusted to the idea of becoming parents.

It was an Olympic year, and Katia and Sergei watched the 1992 Games on their television set in Moscow. It had been four years since their own victory, and so much had happened in that time. In 1988, they had just been close friends, but now they were married and soon-to-be parents. Part of them wished they could compete in the Olympics again one day, but they were happy that they had turned professional. At the time, International Skating Union (ISU) rules dictated that professionals were not allowed to compete in the Olympics. Katia and Sergei had heard that Brian Boitano was drafting a letter to the ISU requesting that professionals be allowed to compete in the next Olympics, which were going to be held in 1994. They did not get their hopes up, though, but instead concentrated on what was certain in their future—parenthood.

Katia was determined that they finish with Stars on Ice, which ended in April. Those three months were extremely hard on her. "Every night I flopped onto my bed, thinking 'Oh this feels great. I'm going to have so much energy tomorrow.' But I never did," she recalled. Marina Zueva, who had left Russia the previous year to live in Canada, was happy to hear the couple's good news. Although the pair had been working with other choreographers, Marina was still very dear to Katia and Sergei. She said that after the baby's birth, she would help Katia skate again. Marina was a mother as well and knew the work that was involved in parenthood. Her son, Fedor Andreev, had been born in 1982—the year that Gordeeva and Grinkov were matched together in Moscow.

Katia's skating friends had a baby shower for her, and she was touched by their generosity. She was surprised that they all knew she was expecting, but her pregnancy was starting to show and the word had spread. They returned to Moscow to enjoy the time off from touring and to prepare to become parents. After learning that the baby would be a girl, they decided to name her Daria. They chose this name because Elena Gordeeva had once said that if she had given birth to a third girl, she would have named her Daria. That summer, Sergei took Katia on a two-week vacation through Switzerland and Greece.

As Katia's September 20 due date approached, she started thinking that perhaps it would be better to have the baby in the United States. Her doctor in Russia had said that because she was so small, Katia would have to

have a cesarean section instead of a natural delivery. In a cesarean section, or "c-section," the doctor performs surgery to remove the baby. Although many women give birth by the cesarean method, the recovery time is substantially longer than that of a natural birth. Katia wanted to return to Stars on Ice and rehearsals began at the end of October; cesarean birth would put the whole season in jeopardy. She believed that she had a better chance of a natural delivery in the United States because doctors there would not have already decided that she was a candidate for a c-section. Paul Theofanous, a friend at IMG, found Gordeeva and Grinkov an obstetrician in Morristown, New Jersey, and rented a

On September 11, 1992, Daria Sergeyevna Grinkova was born. The skaters doted on their tiny towheaded child, seen here with her mother as a three-year-old. "Any time spent with Daria is enjoyable," Gordeeva said in 1998. "It doesn't matter what we do."

condominium where they could live during the last weeks of Katia's pregnancy.

Early in the morning of September 11, Katia started having contractions. When they arrived at the hospital, Sergei believed he was supposed to leave the hospital and come back once the baby was born. In Russia, the father does not participate in the birth. Sergei was in the car when a nurse came out to the parking lot and told him he was needed inside. A short while later, Daria Sergeyevna Grinkova was born. She was a small baby—five pounds, four ounces—but healthy.

Elena Gordeeva came to stay with the new parents. "Mom showed us how to do everything: burp Daria, give her baths, change her clothes," said Katia. "Every day there was some small change. One day she'd move her eyes. The next day she'd move her legs. The first bath. The first smile. All the time we were thanking God that He had brought us such happiness."

At this time, Gordeeva and Grinkov decided to join the Stars on Ice tour again, and had to make a difficult decision about Daria. They needed to earn money, and wanted to skate, but did not want to leave Daria with strangers at their hotels. Their dilemma was resolved when Elena Gordeeva agreed to take care of the baby while they were on the road. "We could quit skating to be with Daria, have no money, live like all Russian people back in Moscow, and someday coach," Gordeeva noted. "Or we could skate and let my mom raise Daria. That was the choice." Although she knew it was the right choice, Katia was sorry to leave her infant daughter.

Because she had a natural delivery, the new mother was able to get back onto the ice just 19 days after Daria was born. At first, skating was hard for Katia. She had been away from the ice for over six months and kept falling on her jumps. To celebrate Daria's birth, choreographer Michael Seibert created a new routine entitled

"Reverie." In the program's beginning, there was a taped introduction by Katia: "I feel very lucky. I am doing what I love to do. I am skating together with [a] man who love[s] me [very] much and I love him very much too. And now we have a baby. I feel like I am [the] luckiest woman in the world." The program focused less on jumps and more on interaction between Sergei and Katia. Their pale blue costumes blended with the ice and their movements seemed to come from deep inside. They held each other and touched even more on the ice than in previous programs, reflecting their love and happiness. Things were going so well in their lives that for perhaps the first time, Katia was truly content with every aspect of her life. There was nothing more she wanted, and good news was about to increase her joy.

Gordeeva and Grinkov were determined to again reach the height of amateur competition in 1994 by winning a second Olympic gold medal.

6

GRAND AND GRACEFUL

IN 1993, THE INTERNATIONAL Skating Union decided to change its rules regarding Olympic competition. Professionals would be allowed to compete in the 1994 Winter Games in Lillehammer, Norway. Now that they were parents, Ekaterina Gordeeva and Sergei Grinkov were unsure whether they had the motivation to skate in, and win, the Olympics. But they decided that they wanted to stand on the Olympic medals podium again, and wrote a letter to the ISU requesting that their amateur status be reinstated.

Katia and Sergei agreed that the best person to create their Olympic program was Marina Zueva. Marina was delighted to work with the pair on their Olympic return. She had been planning a program set to Beethoven's "Moonlight Sonata" for the pair since she left Russia to live in Canada. They decided on the Beethoven piece for the long program, while the short program was set to a Spanish gypsy style of dance music known as flamenco. They also decided to train for the Olympics in Ottawa, Canada, where Marina lived.

First, however, the pair returned to Moscow to see Elena Gordeeva and Daria, and they insisted that Katia's mother and their daughter stay with them in Ottawa while they trained for the Games. It had been months since they had seen their daughter and Katia and Sergei could not believe how quickly the toddler, who was learning to crawl, was growing.

Daria's birth had also brought about a noticeable change in the skating of G & G. Now, more than ever, they were skating as one. "It has been said that their hearts beat in unison," Olympic skater Peggy Fleming noted. Marina was especially delighted with the development in their skating. "You're doing everything I told you so perfectly. It's almost like you were preparing your whole career for this program." Sergei loved the program and felt closer to the music than he had with any other routine.

Appropriately, the theme for "Moonlight Sonata" was man celebrating woman as the mother of all mankind. Rather than wear distracting costumes, the pair decided on very simple navy velvet costumes with a solid white stripe down the front and around the collar. Katia and Sergei were excited to perform the routine in competition at Skate Canada in November 1993. A first place finish at Skate Canada gave them confidence heading into the upcoming Olympic year. This was important, because returning to amateur status meant that the pair would have to qualify for the Games by finishing well in pre-Olympic competitions. When reporters asked Katia why they had decided to compete in the Olympics again, she simply replied, "We wanted to see if we could do it. We wanted to see if we were still good enough."

While they were getting ready for Lillehammer, Grinkov and Gordeeva were faced with the death of yet another loved one when Sergei's sister's boyfriend Dmitri died. He was only in his late thirties. Gordeeva watched her husband comfort his grieving sister, and his words about Dmitri's death helped Katia years later. "Dmitri's all around," Sergei said. "He's not in human form, but he's in this kitchen right now; he's in this bedroom. He can see you and hear you even if you can't see him." In the fall of 1994, Katia's grandfather also passed away, and she vowed that one day she would pick mushrooms with Daria and teach her everything that her diaka had taught her.

Preparation for the Olympics was tougher than it had been in 1988. Although Gordeeva was only 22 and Grinkov 26, most figure skaters are even younger. Katia knew that the Russian pairs, especially, were young and hungry. Gordeeva and Grinkov were able to overcome these younger competitors when they won the Russian national championship in January 1994. It was their first Nationals win since 1987, and it qualified G & G to compete for Russia in the European Championships and the 1994 Winter Olympics.

The European Championships were held in a familiar arena in Copenhagen. Katia and Sergei stayed in the same hotel they had in 1986, when they had competed in their first European Championships. They won the competition with what Gordeeva felt was one of the team's best performances. The victory gave Gordeeva and Grinkov confidence heading into the Olympics.

Meanwhile, the big news in the skating world during 1994 was a man's attack on Nancy Kerrigan. He hit her in the knee with a piece of pipe, and the injury nearly kept her out of the Olympics. Later, the attacker was linked to a fellow skater and Olympic hopeful, Tonya Harding. While the incident left a dark mark on the skating world, it also brought attention to the sport itself. Many new viewers tuned in for Olympic skating that year; as a result, more people would be watching Gordeeva and Grinkov, or "Grand and Graceful" as they were sometimes called, than had when they won in 1988.

Wearing simple costumes, Sergei and Katia perform in the 1994 Olympics. The program, to the music of Beethoven's "Moonlight Sonata," was Sergei's favorite; the theme, man celebrating woman.

Many of the young amateur Olympic skaters welcomed Katia and Sergei back to amateur competition, but others resented their return, believing that G & G were too good. The pair had to ignore these negative comments if they wanted to prove that they still had the competitive drive to win the Olympics. They were better than they had been in 1988, but so was the competition. Canadian pair Isabelle Brasseur and Lloyd Eisler and fellow Russians Natalia Mishkutenok and Artur Dmitriev were also favored for medals.

When the Olympics began, Gordeeva was more nervous than she could ever recall feeling in previous competitions. Remembering her mom, dad, and Daria back home and listening to Marina's advice helped calm her down. "Forget about everyone else. Skate for Sergei," Marina told her. The pair skated their short routine flawlessly and were in first place entering the long program.

Before that all-important routine, Katia vowed that, medal or not, she would remember this Olympic experience and value it more than she had in '88. Life was no longer only about medals and skating. "In Lillehammer I was like a sponge," Katia remembered. "I just wanted to fill myself with a lot of feelings so I [would] remember them forever."

Their performance in the Olympic long program was inspired, every lift high and light, every jump cleanly landed. However, some of their spins were out of sync, and Sergei, who rarely missed an element in competition, singled a double salchow jump. But in spite of these minor errors and near-flawless performances from the Canadian pair Brasseur and Eisler and countrymen Mishkutenok and Dmitriev, eight of the nine judges gave Gordeeva and Grinkov top marks. They soon stood at the top of the podium with their gold medals, as they had in 1988, while the Russian national anthem played.

Although they had won a second gold medal, Sergei was disappointed with his mistake. He now vowed to return to Olympic competition in 1998. "He wanted to compete again, to erase that single blemish from his thoughts," Katia said. "A third Olympic bid. I didn't think I could handle the pressure of another Olympics, but I couldn't say no, because I saw the hope in his eyes."

Unlike their victory at Calgary in 1988, Ekaterina and Sergei celebrated their second gold medal together. They skied with Dmitriev and Mishkutenok, who had won the silver medal, and visited the Russian House, a hospitality center for Russian visitors in Lillehammer, for a party. But the happiest celebration was when Katia and Sergei were reunited with Daria at home in Russia. They had sacrificed so much for their medal, but it had been worth all of the hard work.

The pair opted not to compete in the World Championships after the Olympics. Daria was now one-and-a-half years old, and the family still had no permanent home in the United States. Although Gordeeva and Grinkov had bought a house on impulse in Tampa, Florida, after Daria was born, they realized that they needed to be close to a training facility. Jay Ogden of IMG told Katia and Sergei about a new training center, the International Skating Center, that was being built in Simsbury, Connecticut. Many Eastern European skaters, like Oksana Baiul and Viktor Petrenko, were going to live in Simsbury. When Katia and Sergei saw the condominium complex near the center, they knew they would call the town home. Finally, there was a place for Elena and Daria to stay while they were in America.

Katia and Sergei now not only had a U.S. address, but they also began to be recognized by people, many of whom were not even skating fans. After their second gold medal, *People* magazine named Katia one of the "50

Most Beautiful People in the World." Katia did a photo shoot for the magazine and millions of people read the highly anticipated issue. But she only wished that Sergei had been there with her. The photo, one of very few ever taken of Gordeeva alone while Sergei was alive, hangs in her parents' Moscow apartment.

G & G returned to their professional status and started working on new numbers for the upcoming Stars on Ice tour and the competitive professional skating season. Their new artistic program for the 1994–95 season was set to the music of Rachmaninoff and based on the art of the famous

Despite a minor mistake by Sergei during the long program, G & G won their second Olympic gold medal at the 1994 Games in Lillehammer, Norway. Flanking them on the medals podium are bronze medalists Isabelle Brasseur and Lloyd Eisler (left) of Canada and silver medalists Natalia Mishkutenok and Artur Dmitriev of Russia.

French sculptor Auguste Rodin. The sculptures they
focused on were Rodin's pairs, many of whom were in fan-
tastic positions that were very hard to recreate in real life.
But Marina knew the program was perfect for Gordeeva
and Grinkov. "Sergei's body was like a Greek god's. And
her body is just like a sculpture. You can't add anything to
them. You just take what they have and fix [the moment].
This moment, how people love each other, is perfect. I
wanted to fix this moment for Sergei and Katia forever,
how they love each other," Marina said. To do that, all three
asked themselves, "how would it look like if [the sculp-
tures] came to life?" The result, the program known as
"The Kiss" (after the name of a Rodin sculpture), was
Katia's favorite exhibition program.

For contrast, the other program they chose was an upbeat
number by composer George Gershwin entitled "Crazy For
You." That December the pair skated these two programs to
win their third World Professional Championship.

Right after their win, it was time to tour with Stars on
Ice again. The tour, which began in Boston two days
after Christmas, went to 47 cities in just over three
months. The tour members had become like a second
family to Katia and Sergei. And they were equally loved.
"What sticks in my mind most about [Gordeeva and
Grinkov] was how humble they were," said choreographer
Sandra Bezic. "They never made any demands. They
were always so thankful for everything. They always
thought they were lucky to be in Stars on Ice. I'd look at
them and say we are the ones that are thankful that you
are with us."

While Marina was the pair's choreographer for compe-
titions, Bezic created many of the numbers for Stars on
Ice. She chose the music of Ella Fitzgerald—the song
"The Man I Love"—for the duo's program that season.
The program was an audience favorite. "I wanted to capture
what I watched on a daily basis and the way they looked

at each other," Bezic revealed. "Like lovers stealing kisses in a park. It was a very simple number. I didn't want choreography to get in the way of the relationship. It was the quintessential love song." The song's words were also special to Katia: "Someday he'll come along, the man I love / and he'll be big and strong, the man I love / and when he comes my way I'll do my best to make him stay."

After the tour ended, in April 1995, Katia and Sergei were finally able to return to their condo in Simsbury to relax and be with Daria. Springtime in Simsbury was beautiful. The flowers were in bloom, the days were getting longer, and for a change there was no place the family had to be. Katia's 24th birthday was at the end of May, and Sergei drove her to New York City and bought her a designer handbag. The next morning Sergei made his wife breakfast in bed. Katia was surprised by this gesture because although Sergei was a great skater, he was not a cook. He did not even know how to work the coffeemaker. But by watching Katia in the days leading up to his planned surprise, Sergei managed to learn enough to make toast and coffee, and he added a beautiful bouquet of flowers to the tray. Wanting to remember the moment forever, Katia had Sergei take her picture with the breakfast.

Sergei and Katia in a lighthearted moment on the ice, 1989.

7

SAYING GOOD-BYE

SERGEI HAD REINJURED his back after the Olympics when they were practicing a death spiral. But the 1995–96 season was upon them, and he needed to get healthy so that they could begin learning new programs. Although Marina came to Simsbury to introduce them to their new routine, they could not practice. The back injury was so bad that Sergei could not feel his feet on the ice. So all summer, while Katia skated, her husband worked out, lifted weights, and swam. Although Grinkov was frustrated with his injury and unable to improve as a skater, Katia believed that Sergei grew that summer as a person. "Every afternoon Sergei took Daria for a walk and played with her outside. He was such a good father. He'd become so strong, not only with his muscles, but as a person. More of a father. More of a husband. I felt so proud of him that summer."

For a time, it seemed as if Sergei was getting better. But when they got back on the ice again, he reinjured himself during a spin. The pair was worried, not only about the upcoming competitive and touring season, but also about the contract they had signed with Disney to film an on-ice version of *Pocahontas* in Sun Valley, Idaho. Fortunately, the special did not require Sergei to do much skating. While it was a lot of work, the trip to Sun Valley was also a family vacation. Both Elena and Daria joined them, and the group celebrated Daria's third birthday.

Rather than worry about upcoming competitions, Sergei and Katia instead decided to focus their energy on making it through the 55-city Stars on Ice tour. They rented a condo in Lake Placid for rehearsals and settled in.

On November 17, 1995, they went to see a movie and spent the rest of the night in front of the fireplace. The next day, a Saturday, they walked through the town of Lake Placid and picked up some Christmas presents for Daria. Marina arrived on Sunday afternoon. After rehearsing well into the evening, the three went out for a nice dinner. They talked about costumes, the program, and Daria. Their daughter was with Katia's parents in Simsbury but was going to come out to stay on the 21st. Her arrivals were always eagerly anticipated, not only by her parents but also by the rest of the Stars on Ice cast, who had dubbed Daria's visits "Dasha Day." None of the other cast members had children, and Daria was pampered and adored by everyone. "Tomorrow is a Dasha day!" Scott Hamilton said to Sergei on the morning of the 20th. Sergei threw his arms into the air, not knowing that he would not live to see his daughter again.

As news spread of Sergei's heart attack at the skating rink that afternoon, close friends were stunned. Tom Collins, the skating promoter who had invited Katia and Sergei on their first American tour, thought the news was incorrect. "Are you sure you're [not] talking about someone else, another Russian, not Sergei Grinkov?" he asked the person who told him. But soon he learned the truth: the 28-year-old skater was dead.

Ekaterina comforts Sergei's mother during the funeral service in Moscow.

Because he had lived in two countries, two wakes were held for Sergei. The first was held for his American friends in Saranac Lake, New York. Ekaterina and Sergei's manager and friend, Debbie Nast, made the arrangements, and she was joined there by Katia's parents, the cast of Stars on Ice, and other skating friends. Sergei was dressed in one of his favorite outfits, a black cashmere sweater and pants. Although she had intended to place a letter in Sergei's casket, Katia instead put a picture of Daria inside, hoping it would keep him company on his long journey to his final resting place in Moscow. Guests signed a book and filed in singly for their good-byes. Katia remained in the small room filled with flowers, reflecting on their life together. "It was too perfect, maybe," Katia whispered to her good friend Scott Hamilton. "It's only fairy tales that have happy endings. Everything was too good with me and Sergei for it to end happily."

The first wake in New York helped prepare Katia for the trip to Moscow, where she faced Sergei's grief-stricken family. It also helped her decide what to tell Daria. After consulting with Daria's nursery-school teacher, Ekaterina sat her daughter down and said, "Your father is dead; he's not coming back." While it was very hard for Katia to say these words to her child, she knew it was best to be straightforward and honest. When Daria asked how she could see her father, Ekaterina explained that Sergei was with the angels and that she could visit him in her dreams and picture him in her mind. The explanation seemed to satisfy Daria, who was too young to really understand the permanence of death.

As she traveled to Sergei's second funeral, Katia carried a bouquet of yellow and red flowers that he had picked for her the day before he died. It was the last thing he had given her and although the blossoms were now wilted, she cherished them. The mood in Moscow was not as somber and reverent as it had been in America, but more desperate and frantic. Ekaterina was overwhelmed by people and emotions. Because they had traveled almost constantly during their teenage years, Katia and Sergei had seen little of their families. But even though much of Sergei's extended family had not seen him in years, their grief was still intense.

Nearly 12,000 people attended Sergei's funeral, held at the Central Red Army Club in Moscow on November 25. Sergei was buried at Vagankovsky Cemetery, the resting place of many famous Russians. Although she was moved that Sergei was buried in the famous cemetery and touched by the number of people who had come to say good-bye, the funeral offered little relief to Katia. Immediately following Sergei's death, she even blamed herself, believing that if she had been more attentive and loving she would have noticed warning signs.

The only people who gave her solace during this time were Father Nikolai, the priest who had married Sergei and Katia and had conducted Sergei's funeral service in Moscow, and little Daria, who needed attention, care, and someone to play with her. Listening to Father Nikolai's words reminded Katia of the past and helped her prepare for the future. He reassured her that Sergei's death was not her fault or the result of an angry God wanting to take away what He had so benevolently given. Father Nikolai also told her that she would meet Sergei again. When Ekaterina looked at Daria, she remembered why she had to keep living. Daria, with her father's glowing eyes and wide smile, was their future, and she had to be strong for her daughter.

But at home in Moscow, Katia struggled to find moments of happiness, something to ease the pain and

Hundreds of friends and admirers, including fellow skaters Scott Hamilton and Paul Wylie (pictured at right), paid their last respects at Sergei's funeral in Moscow on November 25, 1995.

empty feelings that Sergei's death had left behind. While people close to her reassured Katia that she need not worry about money or skating ever again, she suddenly decided that skating was exactly what she needed to occupy herself. "It was then that I began to realize that work is the only thing that can help people heal," Ekaterina wrote in *My Sergei*. "At least, it was what could help me heal. I still had skating. I was always a skater first, and to lose both Sergei and skating was more than I could handle." A friend, skater Viktor Petrenko, sent Katia's skates to Moscow, and nearly a month after Sergei's death, Gordeeva felt the ice beneath her feet again. Prior to Sergei's death, nearly every day of her life since age four had involved the ice. The memories of skating with her partner came flooding back, but instead of making her pain more acute, these wonderful memories eventually made her stronger.

The days passed slowly and Katia skated every day. It had been almost 40 days since Sergei's passing, one of two significant milestones in the Russian Orthodox religion. On the ninth day after death, it is believed that the deceased begin their journey to either the gates of Heaven or Hell. On the 40th day, they achieve their own spiritual life and no longer have earthly ties. At this point, it is no longer proper to think of the deceased all of the time. It was just before the 40th day that Katia told Marina about the tribute that their skating friends were arranging in honor of Sergei. They wanted Katia to say a few words at the tribute, but Marina insisted that Ekaterina skate. She would create a new program for her. Ekaterina was unsure at first, she wrote in *My Sergei*:

> It was difficult for me to imagine myself skating in front of people without holding Sergei's hand, without looking into Sergei's eyes, looking only at the audience, trying to fill that huge ice surface all by myself.

But if I were to skate in the exhibition, that was how it would have to be. I wasn't going to skate with another partner. It was inconceivable to think of someone else's arms around me on the ice, touching me. Sergei's was the only hand I had held on the ice since I was eleven years old.

Anxious to know if she should skate, Katia visited Father Nikolai, who urged her to perform for the joy it would bring herself and others. Ekaterina also decided to return to the United States. She did not like the money-hungry Russian entrepreneurs who approached her, and she felt the home that she had created with Sergei needed tending. She spent the New Year's celebration with her family at their dacha, and then she and Daria boarded a plane back to their condominium in Simsbury, Connecticut.

Marina selected the music for Katia's first solo skate— the Adagietto from Gustav Mahler's Symphony No. 5. In the beginning, Katia had trouble skating the program. She felt so weak, so small, so insignificant on the ice without Sergei. Her heart was too heavy and the pain was still fresh. But slowly she got stronger and began to realize that the tribute was the right time to skate solo.

During the months between Sergei's funeral and the skating tribute to his life, Katia found that many people shared her grief. Katia and Daria received cards, letters, flowers, and gifts, and she was grateful for the support. More than ever, she valued her friends and all of the fans— most of whom she had never met—for their sympathy and their words of kindness. "Sometimes it bothers me that people now recognize me only because of tragedy," Katia said. "But I've come to understand that people really care and worry for me. I feel I should say to every person I meet, 'I'm fine, Daria's fine. Life goes on.'"

She wanted the planned tribute to be about hope in the face of death. "The message I will try to send to the people

The audience at the skating tribute to Sergei Grinkov, "A Celebration of a Life," was silent as Ekaterina Gordeeva raised her eyes heavenward, as if she was asking God why He took her husband away.

will be that this is not a story about myself, but about everyone," she told reporters. "For all people who have had their period of time in their life that they went through that was very difficult, when they lost somebody or lost themselves and they have to start over again."

In 1996, after the tribute, Katia found herself swamped with requests for interviews. She appeared on *CBS This Morning*, *Dateline*, *Good Morning America*, *Primetime Live*, and *The Oprah Winfrey Show*. The world found Katia's gracious demeanor and stilted English endearing, but most of all they found her story touching.

Gordeeva also teamed up with *Sports Illustrated* writer E. M. Swift to write a book about her life with Sergei. Swift interviewed Katia several times during the early spring. "[Writing the book] was a huge healing process for me," Katia revealed on *Good Morning America*. "It was difficult, definitely very difficult to go through some part[s], but it was also a lot of fun to go through . . . my life again and remember how great it was."

Her book, entitled *My Sergei: A Love Story*, was written in only 22 days by Swift, based on taped recordings and his interview notes. Katia's English improved markedly over the course of their conversations. As Gordeeva told the story of her life with Sergei, there were tears and laughter. "The one time she got emotional when I wasn't expecting it was when we were talking in general terms about the book," Swift remembered, "and she said that she now had no private life; that by telling her innermost secrets and memories of Sergei, she had abandoned her private life forever."

Despite the loss of privacy, Katia believed the book was for her daughter, who one day will want to know the story of her parents. "I'll make sure that she knows the kind of man her father was, the kind of heart he had." Katia's dedication, written in Russian, reveals her feelings:

I dedicate this book to my Seriozha. To my lover, my husband, the father of my child, a great sportsman and my best friend.

During his short and intense life Sergei managed to give to many people some minutes of beauty. He lived for love and could give it to people because love was his natural state.

I am grateful to Seriozha for every day I lived at his side, for every smile, every kind word.

Seriozha, I'll treasure our wonderful fairy tale which we both lived and I'll tell it to our daughter.

Writing My Sergei: A Love Story *was therapeutic for Ekaterina Gordeeva; she was able to confront her feelings about her husband and his sudden death. When the book was released in November 1996 it became an immediate bestseller.*

My Sergei became an instant *New York Times* bestseller when it appeared in bookstores in November 1996. Reviews of the book were glowing. Allegra Young of *USA Today* wrote that "the autobiography is well-written, reflecting Gordeeva's maturity, talent, and charm that belie her 25 years. She is never overly sentimental about the past or future—the facts are dramatic enough. . . . Perhaps the book's only fault is that it does not come with a video."

As Swift was bringing Ekaterina's story to life, Katia had started skating professionally again. The change from pairs to singles skating was difficult not only emotionally, but also physically. Although Katia had started out as a singles skater, she had not been alone on the ice in over 13 years. All the elements that she had learned as part of a team had to be relearned for solo skating. "It's fairly rare to succeed at both pairs and solo skating," skater Rosalynn Sumners noted in *Good Housekeeping* magazine. "And it's been interesting to see how Katia developed her own style. For many months after she began to skate again, it was hard for those of us who knew Sergei to watch her. It was bizarre and sad without him, and she was left quite raw and vulnerable. But we saw her build her own inner strength."

When reporters asked if she believed she was doing what Sergei would have wanted by skating solo, Katia replied that she was skating for everyone to remember her and Sergei together. "She had this way of unfolding her arms to the back, and you expect her to look back at him—and he's not there," said event producer Jirina Ribbens.

In April, Katia joined the Chrysler Stars on Ice tour in Canada and then skated in Discover Stars on Ice shows in Hawaii, Japan, and Korea. "I can't compare skating alone to skating with someone else," Katia said. "Pairs skating is much more artistic. There are more possibilities to tell a story with two people than one." Her choreographers were now faced with the task of designing solo programs. The routine "Morning," set to the *Peer Gynt Suite* by Edvard Grieg, was delicate and light, with many arm movements and spins that Katia could not perform while she had skated with Sergei. Her pale pink costume with chiffon skirt and satin top matched the mood of the program, which told of the rebirth that comes with the morning. Katia managed to tell the story alone.

Before his death, Katia and Sergei had learned that they were going to be inducted into the World Figure Skating Hall of Fame in Colorado. All of the 600 people at the ceremony on May 12, 1996, were thinking of Sergei. Katia tightly held the hands of Kristi Yamaguchi and Scott Hamilton, two of her closest skating friends, while a video of G & G was played.

After the induction, Katia began shooting the Walt Disney television special "Beauty and the Beast: A Concert on Ice." Katia portrayed the Beauty, Belle, while good friend Viktor Petrenko played the Beast. It was the first time Katia had skated with anyone other than Sergei, but the fact that it was with Viktor made the job much easier. Scott Hamilton, Lloyd Eisler, and JoJo Starbuck also starred in the hour-long special that aired that fall.

While Katia was as busy as she had ever been touring with Sergei, she almost always found herself occupied by thoughts of him. The condominium in Simsbury was full of reminders of the life they had shared, and Katia could not bear to put away his things. Photographs of the two graced every room, Sergei's dog-eared Russian novels lay on the shelves, and his clothes hung in the closet. "I have left everything just the way it was before," Katia told *People* magazine in the spring of 1996. "I can't touch anything." The memories of their times there haunted her, but she could not bear to leave their home. "He would never come into a room and not touch me in some way," she said. "All the time, we would never cross without touching our hands or giving a kiss." Katia had decided to continue skating because that helped her feel strong and confident. She knew that she needed to live for the present and not for the past.

On September 13, 1996, Katia competed for the first time as a singles skater at the Northwestern Mutual Life World Team Championship. She decided that the format of a team competition was the best arena in which to begin competing again. "I feel that I am not alone," she explained. "Even though they are on the other side of the boards, still I know [my teammates] will support me." Her two programs were both beautifully skated, but Katia struggled with her jumps. When asked what was the hardest thing about being a singles skater, Katia responded, "Everything. Just to start and to learn jumps and spins and to go through the program alone, because I'm used to someone lifting me and some parts of the program I'm not on my feet. I have to be on my feet through my program now." Although the Russian team came in last behind the other three teams—Europe, the United States, and Canada—the evening was filled with excitement as a new chapter opened in Katia's life.

Ekaterina Gordeeva skates solo with Stars on Ice in November 1996, a year after her husband's death.

8

SKATING FOR SERGEI

IN NOVEMBER 1996, as the first anniversary of Sergei's death approached, 25-year-old Katia drew solace from her friends. She had become especially close to some of the other skaters on the tour. "When Sergei died, I was out there all alone," she told *Newsweek* magazine. "I didn't have any close friends, not even a close girlfriend. . . . This has been some kind of new experience to find out what friendship is all about." As rehearsals for the 1996–97 season of Stars on Ice began, the cast joined hands with Katia on the ice, in the very spot where Sergei had collapsed. Prayers were said, and Katia handed each of her precious friends a small blue box with a white ribbon from the famous jewelry store Tiffany's. Inside each box was a silver star key chain inscribed with the word "Smile." "I wouldn't have made it through without you guys," Katia told them.

In 1997, Katia felt stronger than she had in a long time. She finally felt ready to leave the condominium that she and Sergei had shared and move into a new house. She bought a five-bedroom house in Simsbury, big enough for her entire family to come and stay. "Our house is now our home and it is always full of people, lots of love, and laughter," Katia said in the summer of 1998.

Fans of G & G were ecstatic to see Katia back as a solo performer with the tour in the United States and Canada. One of her programs, "If It Takes Forever" from the French musical film *The Umbrellas of Cherbourg*, was an instant hit with audience members. The movie tells the story of a 16-year-old French woman and 20-year-old French man who, although they are in love, are parted when he is drafted into the army. "The character I want to show is a woman who is in love with a man but unfortunately they can't be together," Katia told the fan club newsletter *Grace & Gold*, which is dedicated to the memory of G & G, as well as to following Katia's solo career.

On March 18, 1997, the skating community got another unpleasant surprise when Scott Hamilton, the 1984 Olympic gold medalist and originator of the Stars on Ice tour, was diagnosed with testicular cancer. Hamilton dropped out of the tour and underwent chemotherapy treatment over the next few months, followed by surgery to remove the cancer in June. While Hamilton was recovering, the entire cast held their breath, hoping that Scott would beat the cancer. Fortunately, Katia had other projects to help keep her mind off her friend's troubles. Back in Simsbury to film an Arts & Entertainment network special entitled "The Art of Russian Skating," Katia learned that CBS was interested in turning *My Sergei* into a two-hour, prime-time documentary. The movie would include clips of G & G performances, interviews with friends and family, and dramatic re-creations of scenes in their life not caught on film, such as their first kiss in the sauna. Both Katia and Daria were asked to participate in the project and appear on film. Thrilled with the news, Katia agreed to the project and wanted to make the special an accurate depiction of her love for Sergei.

Gordeeva is able to smile during an interview as she talks about the television program based on My Sergei. *The two-hour, prime-time documentary included clips of G & G performances, interviews with friends and family, and dramatic re-creations of scenes from their lives. "My Sergei" aired on February 4, 1998, which would have been Sergei Grinkov's 31st birthday.*

Before the filming of "My Sergei" was finished in the summer of 1997, Katia was asked to film another television special, this one for children. "Snowden on Ice" was an original musical holiday show about a young, single mother who returns to her old hometown. Scott Hamilton had undergone a successful surgery to remove the cancer and was set to play the narrator Scootch. The cast also included Josee Chouinard and Kurt Browning. Katia's agreement to star in the television show came after she signed a contract with the show's sponsor, the department-store chain Target. "Ekaterina's energy, courage, and lovable personality make a perfect match for Target," said John Pellegrene, executive vice-president of marketing for the Minneapolis-based chain. "Snowden on Ice" was the first project under her multiyear deal, which also includes commercials, product endorsements, and in-store appearances.

Filming "Snowden on Ice" was a new experience for Gordeeva. Although figure skating can be considered a form of acting, there is no dialogue, unlike a television special. "When you're skating, you feel more comfortable because you've been trained for competition," she told *People* magazine. "But to memorize lines, it's difficult!"

The special, which aired on November 28, 1997, starred Gordeeva as a single mother, Kate, who returns with her young daughter to her childhood home, Albert Pond, after a long absence. Since a skating fall 10 years earlier, Kate, a successful children's book author, has developed an aversion to the single most popular pastime in the town—ice skating. But upon returning to Albert Pond, she remembers a story her deceased Uncle Albert used to tell her about Snowden the magical snowman. The memory of Snowden helps her overcome her fear of skating and helps her daughter Lizzie adjust to life in her new hometown.

Because the special was filmed in August, during Daria's summer vacation from school, the four-and-a-half-year-old was allowed to star on-screen with her mom as Lizzie. One thing that surprised Katia about her young daughter was her ability to take direction and apply it to her performance. After the experience, Katia suspected that Daria one day might be successful in show business.

But it is important to Katia that Daria follow her own desires. Because Ekaterina had showed promise as a skater at an early age, Soviet policy dictated that she become a skater. Luckily, she enjoyed her career, but she could have just as easily resented the profession. Daria, on the other hand, will be allowed to decide what she wants to do with her life, and Gordeeva will have fun being her mother. "Any time spent with Daria is enjoyable," Gordeeva confided. "It doesn't matter what we do."

Katia expressed her wishes for her daughter, and the lessons that she herself learned as a child, in a 1998 book called *A Letter for Daria*. Whereas *My Sergei* had focused on her past with Sergei, *A Letter for Daria* focused on her future with their daughter. Written with Antonina W. Bouis, the book includes many personal photos of Daria and Katia, drawings by Daria, and lessons written for Daria, with chapters such as "My Babushka," "Your Babushka," "Religion," "Family Traits," and "When You Grow Up." Manager Debbie Nast said of the book, "It's basically stories about her childhood and lessons she's learned from her parents, her mother, and her grandmother. [It is] sort of instilling that in Daria and how important it is that she has choices, that she can make her own choices in life." "Daria, my little Dasha," the book begins, "I am writing this book for you. I hope it will bring a smile to your face more than once when you learn to read it by yourself. You are my daughter, my baby, the dearest person in the world to me."

"I wasn't sure if I should do [the book] or not," Gordeeva told *International Figure Skating* magazine. "But then I met Russian writer Antonina Bouis. . . . She said, 'Let's talk about just Russian tradition, why Russian people are enjoying to have grandmothers around their kids. Why it's important for them.' And then I just thought that that's really something to talk about."

But before the book hit shelves in April 1998, Gordeeva witnessed the incredible reaction to the television docudrama "My Sergei." It aired on February 4, 1998—which would have been Sergei Grinkov's 31st birthday—just several days prior to the start of the Winter Olympics in Nagano, Japan, the games in which Sergei had wanted to compete. Gordeeva was very proud of the work and happy that it was well received by the public. "Katia is a very special, strong individual," Laura Ouziel, the associate producer of the docudrama, said. "Her input has been invaluable, her warmth and generosity of spirit is obvious. She opened up her home to us and gave us whatever we needed to ensure that we would produce the best possible piece of work."

Just after the special aired, Katia traveled to Nagano, Japan, to be a part of the CBS team of commentators. While she spent significant time in the studio commentating about the pairs' and women's competitions, Katia also attended many of the events, especially skating. When Sergei's longtime friend Artur Dmitriev won the pairs competition with a new partner, Oksana Kazakova, he looked up into the stands and waved to Katia. Also, during that month Katia and Daria's "Why Milk" ads, featuring mother and daughter encouraging people to drink milk, debuted. In the ad, Gordeeva said she drank milk for something "every skater needs. Strong ankles."

Besides her extremely busy life off the ice, Katia also found the time to tour with the 1997–98 Stars on Ice tour and compete in professional skating competitions. Marina Zueva and Katia developed three new routines for the season: "Smile," "Three Preludes," and "Brazilian Bacchiana No. 5."

Gordeeva starred with Scott Hamilton in the 1997 CBS special "Snowden on Ice." The program also featured the acting debut of her daughter, Daria.

"'Smile' is dedicated to Scott Hamilton to express my gratitude for being a part of his show 'Upside Down Special on Ice,'" Katia explained in *Grace & Gold*. "The second program to Gershwin's music is quite new for my image. The program consists of different moods—cheerful, funny—and also gives me a chance for improvisation. The third program, 'Bacchiana No. 5,' portrays what we call in Russia 'flying soul.' Each human being has a dream to fly, but of course cannot, but the soul can."

Although Katia was still having problems with the consistency of her jumps, she was gradually becoming used to being on the ice alone and was growing stronger in her solo efforts. At the World Professional Championships in December 1997, Katia came in second behind Kristi Yamaguchi, and the Associated Press noted, "Ekaterina Gordeeva, in one of her best performances since becoming a singles skater, performed a warm but technically less demanding routine to 'Smile' to place second behind Kristi Yamaguchi with 97.5 points." The achievement was especially notable because Yamaguchi, like all the others who competed, had been a singles skater for many years.

In March 1998, Katia and Target Stores introduced a new fragrance simply called "Katia." In a press release, Ekaterina said, "It's very exciting to have my own perfume. We worked together to make sure it would be very beautiful. I wanted to make sure it would be a fragrance I'd love to wear." The perfume is a floral scent with citrus undertones, and the bottle, a pale blue and pink abstract interpretation of a skater, arms outstretched performing a spin, is as beautiful as the scent. The perfume line includes body lotion, bath foam, shower cream, body mist, soap gift sets, potpourri, and scented candles. Katia is also Target's spokesperson for St. Jude's Research Hospital; in May 1999 she will dedicate a garden in Sergei's honor at the

Although she still thinks about Sergei, Ekaterina Gordeeva has chosen not to dwell on her loss, but instead to move ahead with her life. The skater is confident that this is what her husband would have wanted. "I am cautiously stepping into the future with my mind set on becoming, if not happier, at least wiser in life," she said at the end of My Sergei.

new Target House, a home for long-term patients and their families to stay in while receiving treatment at the hospital.

In April, after she finished the Stars on Ice season, Katia began a book tour, signing copies of *A Letter for Daria*. At every appearance, supportive fans were there to greet her. Sometimes hundreds swarmed the bookstore, waiting in line for hours for an autograph and a handshake from Katia.

Gordeeva's popularity and influence in the sport as both a pairs and singles skater was acknowledged when she was named one of *International Figure Skating* magazine's "25 Most Influential Names in Figure Skating." "I never knew where life would take me," she told the magazine. "Life was very good to me, and it takes me all around the world. . . . I'm a figure skater. I'm a mother of a wonderful daughter, Daria."

While Katia spends most of the year in America touring, she still returns every year to her birthplace. In the summer she and Daria vacation at the family dacha with her parents. "As much as I love living in the U.S., I will always have a Russian soul," she admits. "It is something you are born with and are always proud of." In this way, she is still connected with Sergei Grinkov, whom she continues to think of every day. "First of all he was a man, then he was a skater," she said.

She hopes to fall in love again one day, and Daria asks to have a little brother or sister. "It's very hard for me to take anything seriously. Even though I know that I should," she told *Good Housekeeping* magazine. "I know that Daria needs a father, needs a man. But it is a decision I must make on my own and it's very difficult. Maybe in time I can be more relaxed. I will always think of Sergei as the first man. I'm always comparing. It will take a long time. We weren't perfect. We had problems. But still, he was the only man for me."

Over the years, fans and fellow skaters have gotten

used to seeing Katia alone on the ice without Sergei as she continues to compete and star in skating specials such as 1998's "The Snowden, Raggedy Ann & Andy Holiday Show." But they will never forget the beauty of G & G's skating. "Their time and their space is separate from the rest of skating history," Scott Hamilton once observed.

Daria has begun to know who her father was and understand, all too painfully, the concept of death. In *A Letter for Daria,* Katia wrote, "the other day when we were reading 'The Little Mermaid' again, at the part where it says that only human souls can go up to heaven and mermaids can't, you said, 'See that's like Papa. He lives in Heaven. With the angels.'"

Ekaterina Gordeeva looks back on the figure skating accomplishments of which she is most proud and happy—their two Olympic medals and her part in "A Celebration of a Life"—and the day when Sergei died. "No matter what lies ahead, the best years of my life will have been with Sergei," Katia said. But she has since realized that she is not alone in having lost the most important person in her life. She also knows what pain is, and this awareness has made her appreciate happiness more. "[People] must find ways to believe in themselves. To find someone to live for. When everything feels like it is broke[n] inside, you have to get up from your knees and ask God for some help. You can have a life now."

CHRONOLOGY

1971   Born Ekaterina Alexandrovna Gordeeva on May 28, in Moscow, U.S.S.R.

1975   Joins the Central Red Army Club and begins ice skating

1982   Paired with 15-year-old Sergei Mikhailovich Grinkov

1983   Sergei and Katia place fifth at the Junior World Championships in Sapporo, Japan

1984   Sergei and Katia win the Junior World Championships in Colorado Springs, Colorado

1986   G & G place second in the Soviet National Championships held in St. Petersburg, U.S.S.R.; place second at the European Championships in Copenhagen, Denmark; win the gold medal at the World Championships in Geneva, Switzerland

1987   Sergei and Katia win the Soviet National Championships in Vilnius, Lithuania; win the World Championships in Cincinnati, Ohio; join skating promoter Tom Collins on their first American skating tour; Katia injures her head after a fall and is hospitalized

1988   Sergei and Katia win the European Championships in Prague, Czechoslovakia; win gold medal at the Olympic Games in Calgary, Alberta, Canada; share their first kiss on New Year's Eve

1989   Sergei and Katia win the World Championships held in Paris, France

1990   G & G win the European Championships held in St. Petersburg, U.S.S.R.; win the World Championships held in Halifax, Nova Scotia, Canada; turn professional; Sergei gets title to apartment and proposes to Katia

1991   Katia and Sergei marry on April 28; begin touring with Stars on Ice; win World Professional Figure Skating Championships in Landover, Maryland; win Challenge of Champions in Oslo, Norway

1992   Katia gives birth to daughter Daria Sergeyevna Grinkova on September 11; G & G win World Professional Figure Skating Championships in Landover, Maryland

1993   Sergei and Katia request reinstatement of amateur status February 10; win Skate Canada competition in Ottawa, Ontario, Canada

1994   Katia and Sergei win Russian National Championships in St. Petersburg, Russia, to qualify for 1994 Olympics; win European Championships held in Copenhagen, Denmark; win gold medal at the Winter Olympic Games in Lillehammer, Norway; Katia named one of *People* magazine's "50 Most Beautiful People in the World"; return to professional status; move to Simsbury, Connecticut; win World Professional Championships

1995   G & G win Challenge of Champions in Tokyo, Japan; Sergei Grinkov dies on November 20 in Lake Placid, New York; funeral held November 25 in Moscow, Russia

1996   Skates in tribute to Sergei, "A Celebration of a Life," on February 27; collaborates on book *My Sergei: A Love Story* with E. M. Swift; G & G inducted into World Figure Skating Hall of Fame on May 12; Katia competes in first competition after Sergei's death at the World Team Championships held in Milwaukee, Wisconsin

1997   Signs endorsement contract with Target Stores; stars in CBS television special "Snowden on Ice" with daughter Daria

1998   CBS television documentary "My Sergei" airs prior to Winter Olympic Games; joins the CBS news team in Nagano, Japan, to provide Olympic skating commentary; develops perfume line "Katia" with Target Stores; writes *A Letter for Daria* with Antonina W. Bouis; appears in CBS television special "The Snowden, Raggedy Ann & Andy Holiday Show"; makes line of television commercials for Target

1999   The Sergei Grinkov Memorial Garden opens at Target House in Memphis, Tennessee

FURTHER READING

Good Morning America interview. ABC Television. Fall 1996.

Gordeeva, Ekaterina, with E. M. Swift. *My Sergei: A Love Story*. New York: Warner Books, 1996.

Gordeeva, Ekaterina, with Antonina W. Bouis. *A Letter for Daria*. Boston: Little, Brown and Company, 1998.

"Gordeeva Right on Target." *International Figure Skating*. March/April 1998.

Kantrowitz, Barbara and Anne Longley. "Beyond the Tears." *People*, March 25, 1996.

"My Sergei." Documentary. CBS Television. February 4, 1998.

Pincus, Aileen. "Doctors link skater's death to genetic defect." Cable News Network. June 28, 1996.

Plummer, William. "Soulmates on Ice." *People*, December 11, 1995.

Popescu, Julian. *Russia*. Philadelphia: Chelsea House Publishers, 1998.

Powell, Joanna. "Everything Reminds Me of Sergei." *Good Housekeeping*, November 1997: pp. 104–107.

Ryan, Tim. "Going It Alone." *Honolulu Star-Bulletin*. April 6, 1996.

Smith, Beverley. *A Year in Figure Skating*. Toronto: McClelland & Stewart, 1996.

Starr, Mark. "Solo But Not Alone." *Newsweek*, December 23, 1996.

Swift, E. M. "A Magical Twosome." *Sports Illustrated*, February 29, 1988.

Young, Allegra. "Skaters' Love Resonates Throughout 'My Sergei.'" *USA Today*. September 8, 1997.

APPENDIX

SUPPORT GROUPS FOR LOSS OF A SPOUSE

The Beginning Experience
305 Michigan Ave.
Detroit, Michigan 48226
Phone (313) 965-5110
Fax (313) 965-5557

To Live Again
P.O. Box 415
Springfield, PA 19064
Phone: (610) 353-7740

They Help Each Other Spiritually (THEOS)
717 Liberty Ave.
1301 Clark Building
Pittsburgh, PA 15222
Phone (412) 471-7779

SUPPORT GROUPS FOR CHILDREN WHO HAVE LOST A PARENT

The Compassionate Friends National Office
P.O. Box 3696
Oak Brook, IL 60522-3696
Phone (708) 990-0010
Fax (708) 990-0246

Rainbows
1111 Tower Road
Shaumburg, IL 60173-4305
Phone: (800) 266-0120
Fax (847) 310-0120

The Dougy Center
3903 S.E. 52nd St.
P.O. Box 86582
Portland, OR 97286
Fax (503) 775-5683

INDEX

PICTURE CREDITS

Anne E. Hill holds a B.A. in English from Franklin and Marshall College, where she wrote for the Franklin and Marshall College magazine and was a member of Phi Beta Kappa. She has written a biography of Denzel Washington as well as *Female Firsts in Their Fields: Broadcasting and Journalism* for Chelsea House Publishers. She lives in Wayne, Pennsylvania, with her husband, George.

James Scott Brady serves on the board of trustees with the Center to Prevent Handgun Violence and is the Vice Chairman of the Brain Injury Foundation. Mr. Brady served as Assistant to the President and White House Press Secretary under President Ronald Reagan. He was severely injured in an assassination attempt on the president, but remained the White House Press Secretary until the end of the administration. Since leaving the White House, Mr. Brady has lobbied for stronger gun laws. In November 1993, President Bill Clinton signed the Brady Bill, a national law requiring a waiting period on handgun purchases and a background check on buyers.